Stop Floating, Start Swimming

Refresh Your Reality

by Unlocking Life's Secret Codes

Peter James Barkley

Stop Floating, Start Swimming

NETKANDI
MEDIA & PUBLISHING

Netkandi Media & Publishing

G10 Worth Corner
Turners Hill Road
Crawley
West Sussex
RH10 7SL

www.NetKandi.Media

ISBN-13: 978-1519506375

Dedication

For all my Friends & Family for always being there and for inspiring me every day, special mention to Windy, Bono, Shanno, Simmo, Will, Smythy, Leeo, Kieran, James, Branchy, Chris, Rogers, CT, Pelly & Mike.

To my for Sister for putting up with me, my Step Dad for raising me like his own son, my Nan & Granddad for being inspirational guides of wisdom and for my Nephew Jack and My Nieces Rosie & Lillie for being daily reminders of what life is all about.

Finally to my Mum, the most Loving and dignified person I know...Everything I am I owe to you.

All of you will always be in my heart

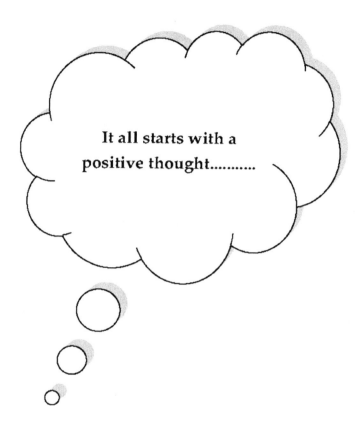

Table of Contents

Readers Tasks

To Do List

Preface
> i. Contract Talks

Introduction
> ii. Challenge – Defining Moments
> iii. Warm Up Task - Mind over Matter
> **iv.** Exam Time

Code 1
> v. Challenge - How do You Feel?
> vi. Task - Goals

Code 2
> vii. Challenge - Time for a Physical
> viii. Task - Fun Times

Code 3
> **ix.** Task – Reality Bites
> x. Challenge - The Mona Lisa

Code 4
> **xi.** Task - Positive People

Code 5
> **xii.** Task - No Regrets

Recap Quiz

Preface

Let's have a talk about the real world...

As a teacher, I would consider myself inept at my job if I was unable to impart some meaningful knowledge to others. The knowledge I wish to share with you goes far beyond the classroom. I truly believe I can inspire anyone of any age to make a positive change to their life.

I didn't plan to teach, by any means. In fact, I hated school as a child and I only really wanted to play football. It was my purpose. I would awake before school to play on my estate with friends, and the game would then occupy my mind all day. As soon as the school bell sounded, I would rush home to continue our game until total darkness had descended on our small patch of grass in Surrey, England. As I reflect on this period of my life, I now understand that football was the first true passion of mine; therefore, it was the first time I was willing to pursue a feeling originating from within my heart. I attempted to overcome all the challenges associated with this deep desire to play the sport professionally.

This dream didn't come to fruition, but thankfully

it did propel me in another direction. I promptly found a new passion working within sport, helping to motivate both young and old people. Over time, I discovered that people connected with me if I displayed energy and enthusiasm, and this connection allowed positive life changes to occur. I started delivering sports coaching sessions in schools and communities with the sole aim of inspiring the past, present and future generations to become more active. Eventually, my skill set evolved and I honed the aptitude required to teach physical education lessons, covering all areas of sport, fitness and wellbeing, to young people in England. I have discovered that the best teachers, and people for that matter, are reflective individuals.

Teaching has taught me to be brave, and to assess my strengths and weaknesses both inside and outside of the classroom. I am not afraid to make mistakes or, indeed, admit that I haven't done things correctly. I am not too proud to apologise. As a reflective thinker, I have been capable of reevaluating my life on numerous occasions; this has enabled me to redefine myself and learn to accept my faults. Faults, errors and mistakes are all part of our personal development and, as you will shortly discover, they can all generate a positive response. Nonetheless, nobody is perfect and there is a huge comfort in knowing and reminding yourself of this fact.

Throughout my teaching career, if I witnessed an opportunity to improve someone's day, or life, with an "outside the box" statement or life lesson, I would seize the moment. It has always been my theory that a child will remember one totally unique and exceptional moment over years of monotonous ones. Think back to your childhood—you probably remember that one truly inspiring teacher who did things a little differently, and equally that truly terrible teacher who struggled to control your class. But how about some of the other teachers or lessons!? Nope, me neither … What's the point of teaching if you can't enthuse, engage and inspire?

I was once teaching a rugby lesson on a playing

field while my colleague Mike was also teaching a Year 7 hockey lesson on the nearby artificial pitch. Around thirty minutes into both our lessons, a loud cheer interrupted my train of thought. As I turned to find the source of this merriment, I witnessed forty pupils riding their hockey sticks like witches' brooms. The pupils appeared to be chasing a small yellow tennis ball. I looked a little closer and I could see some sponge balls being thrown in what resembled a bizarre game of dodgeball. I stopped my Year 11 lesson five minutes early and walked them over to Mike's lesson. All the students from my rugby lesson stood and watched in amazement as this particular group of eleven-year-olds enjoyed the time of their lives. As the lesson came to its natural conclusion, I asked Mike to enlighten my class as to the sport he was teaching and where I could find this particular lesson on the curriculum: **"If you don't know, I feel sorry for you,"** he said as he smiled and walked away. He then beckoned his class over with the wave of his hand. As the Year 7 class hurriedly walked by my class, all red-cheeked and full of enthusiasm, they shouted in unison: **"We were playing QUIDDITCH! DUH!!"** Everyone, myself included, erupted with laughter; some of the Year 11s even started rolling around on the floor, smiles painted on their faces from ear to ear.

The significance of this story is that I remember it. I am able to recall it amongst thousands of lessons I have taught. More importantly, the pupils all remembered this moment. The Year 7s felt amazing about themselves; a younger year group is not normally noticed by the "top dogs" in any school, and they subsequently received high-fives as they wandered between lessons. I love people like Mike and find them truly mesmerizing. I surround myself with people who possess a similar mindset, one of growth and progress. People who feel that life is there for the taking, and they are prepared to push the boundaries to discover unique procedures and methods to acquire results.

I have been inspired by various people throughout my life, and all of them hold a special place in my heart and mind. My experiences have guided me to believe in the power of positivity and the daily pursuit of opportunities to boost the self-esteem of another person. I have conversed with people from all walks of life and of varied ages. I have discovered that adversity has played a major role in most people's lives. It is the response to this adversity that is interesting, for it is this response that eventually defines your character. Haven't you ever wanted to live a life comparable to the likes of Indiana Jones, Robin Hood or even Batman? I guarantee that overcoming adversity is a key theme in your favourite film, book or computer game. With a modified perspective on life, you truly can become the hero of your own story.

In my working life, a pupil knew they were in for a little pearl of wisdom from Mr Barkley if they ever heard the phrase, **"I want to talk to you about the real world..."** The intention of the conversation that preceded this statement would be to inspire a change. The life lessons discussed consisted of certain morals or values that I believed in. Little did I know that these conversations would eventually evolve into life codes—codes that, if followed, will transform your life as they did mine. These five codes became forcefully evident in my darkest hour, at a time when I was physically and mentally broken. I had hit complete and utter rock bottom. I was overweight, unhappy, and riddled with stress and anxiety so intensely that I had developed alopecia (bald patches) in both my hair and beard. Yet here I was, offering life advice to students. Now it was time for me to reflect inwardly on my own circumstances. I couldn't envision a way out, until one day I decided to ask myself a series of questions:

- What is my purpose?

- What do I enjoy doing?

- Where is my life going?

- What would make me happy?

- What am I going to reflect on and be proud of?

- How am I going change things?

The answers cemented the conception of the five life codes, codes that in hindsight I was unwittingly already delivering to students within my "real world" conversations. You may have witnessed a code follower in action—they appear to have an unnerving drive and focus; if they get knocked down seven times, they'll stand up eight. If you have picked up this book, then maybe you are one of them, or desire to be. The five codes you are about to discover work, and that is why I have decided to share them with you. However, you must remember that success, or failure for that matter, does not occur overnight and it is merely a process of smaller actions. It is the consistency of these actions that become habits that eventually create our characters and perspective on life. Maybe now is the time to stop merely surviving and to start thriving, time to start swimming...

Written Agreement

We're nearly there, but before you proceed, please sign and complete the contractual agreement below:

I (Name) .... Promise to complete all the task's and challenges (Including Homework) found within these pages to the best of my ability. I will not continue reading until the task at hand is complete, even if this takes longer than expected. If I am reading this as an EBook, I will use a notebook to complete all work set (Including writing this agreement on Page 1) I will read this book with an open mind.

Signed..

Date...

Print Name...

Witnessed by:

Peter James Barkley

Welcome to the Real World

"All the adversity I've had in my life, all my troubles and obstacles has strengthened me... You may not realize it when it happens, but a kick in the teeth may be the best thing in the world for you." (Walt Disney)

Ernie the Eel

"Swim, Ernie, swim!" The rest of group shouted from the side of the pool as Ernie slowly sunk to the bottom. His self-belief was sinking almost as fast he was, as his heavy, sodden clothes continued to lower him deeper and deeper beneath the surface of the water. The sight and sounds of the onlooking group gradually became blurred and muffled as Ernie peered upwardly to the top of the pool, tiny bubbles of oxygen escaping from his tightly clasped lips. He started to feel physically weak and his legs once again turned to that all-too-familiar jelly-like sensation; however, mentally he felt a sense of peace and calm in these moments when most would feel panic. Suddenly a large metal rod pierced through the stillness of the water and he latched onto it for dear life, literally. As he was sharply pulled to the surface, he could hear the laughter now echoing around the humid poolside. This fifteen-year-old boy had failed once again.

Ernie spent the most part of the intensive four-week training course sinking to the bottom of the pool before being pulled to the surface, only to be laughed at by the others. It was understandable in many ways; swimming was just a minor requirement in becoming part of the British Navy. However, every failure made Ernie want to achieve his goal more. He could have easily quit and thrown in the towel (or had the towel thrown at him). He refused. After numerous extra sessions outside of his regular training hours, he found that he was able to float on the surface of the water. It was a major achievement for Ernie; after all, the instructor had been calling him "The Human Anchor" since Day 2 of the training programme.

Floating started to become easy work to him, so much so that he had totally forgotten what it was like to feel the tiles on the pool's bottom, the sting of the water on his eyes and, of course, the muffled sounds of laughter. His new nickname became "Ernie Buoy" as he floated and drifted along the surface of the water. Floating gradually became treading water and, with an additional four weeks of training, treading water eventually developed into a front crawl. Swimming soon became second nature for Ernie, and he quickly surpassed the ability of all those who had once laughed at him. For the rest of the crew did not need to train as hard in the early stages—they were content with their ability—but Ernie did, and his work ethic and dedication did not cease once he could finally glide across the water. He trained and trained day in, day out; in fact, swimming became a true life passion of his.

Occasionally, he would dive to the bottom of the pool and rest there for a few seconds, feeling the rigid tiles, the sting of the water on his eyes, and take a moment of silence to contemplate his journey and progress.

When he retired from the Navy, Ernie passed his passion on to others and became a first-class swimming instructor for the British Navy Training School. His greatest strength was being able to relate to the journey from the bottom to the top of the pool.

Ernie was a true inspiration, a code follower and my granddad. Throughout his life, he demonstrated all that can be accomplished from life's lessons, if you are prepared to work hard and endeavour through adversity.

Life Lessons

The real world starts the moment you leave school at sixteen years of age. You may be going on to college or an apprenticeship, but in my eyes, you are still entering into the real world. You have increased independence, you are free to travel, and you will start to pay bills and experience new relationships. Unfortunately, at this age, many of us self-define and decide who we are as people, and this internal image shapes the rest of our lives. What age were you when you declared, **"This is who I am, this is what I stand for, this is what I like doing"**? If this was at sixteen, then maybe it's time to rethink the way in which you perceive yourself. We all have a self-definition and this is used as a moral compass for our characters and, therefore, our life choices.

Challenge

What defines you?

Take a few minutes to list 10 things that define who you are.

This is a difficult task and you may not have been

able to think of ten things. Interesting, the majority of people are unable to define themselves, yet they could easily define a friend or family member. To move forward and to progress, we must be self-aware. Take a good look at your list—can you see a description of character traits and core values, or the names of possessions? Have you cited a job title, named brands or even the type of car you drive? Who you are materialises from within, and is not determined by what's outside. If possessions or looks define you, then you are leading a shallow existence, but don't fear—there is time to change. It's good to take some time to look internally and assess what we stand for as individuals, but as we start to become reflective thinkers we must also assess when we created this definition. At what age did you decide to define yourself? Should this definition last a lifetime, or does it need refreshing? When did you decide that you are a "shy," or alternatively, a "confident" person, and how has this internalised view of yourself impacted your responses in certain situations? Your self-image at sixteen or eighteen years old should not be used to dictate your adult life; similarly, nor should your job title.

The real world can be a daunting place as you

attempt to fit in to society while upholding your preconceived self-image. The safety net of school, college and of a structured life has ended. The familiar faces of those teachers that you loathed or loved for the middle years of your teens are no more; they no longer have any power over you (barring job references), and the truth is, most of them will only having a fleeting memory of you. However, you will always remember your teachers as they appeared when you were taught by them. Teachers, lecturers, tutors and sports coaches are frozen in time within our memories. I can recall certain situations in my mind from my own school days as a pupil, and the teachers that taught me remain unchanged by the passing of time. Around fifteen years after I had left school I saw one of my favourite P.E. teachers; he looked so old that I barely recognized him. He caught my eye in a shopping centre car park and I took the opportunity to say hello, unsure if he would recognise me. **"Mr Williams, how are you doing, sir?"** Even at thirty years old, I still referred to him as "sir." **"I'm all right, Pete. Your lot were OK, actually; it was just the rest of those little buggers!"** he replied and then slowly walked away. Initially, I laughed, yet his expression remained as stern as it once did when our class would become unruly during his old teaching days. **"Bloody hell ... how am I going to feel after thirty years of teaching?"** I thought to myself as the interaction faded.

I analysed this for a week or so and then one day it clicked: his experiences won't define mine. I will teach the only way I know how ... my way. My self-image and self-definition are totally unique to me, so it goes with reason to assume that my life experiences will be different. Most of the time in life we are forced to follow a set pathway or route—methods of doing things that have been repeated for many years or even decades, consistently producing the same result or outcome. Who decides on the systems that we must follow and adhere to!? People that make a lasting impact on the world have formed their own set of life rules, have created a strong self-image and have eagerly pushed the boundaries that society has established.

Environmental Change

A key turning point for you, the reader, as you progress through this book will be the concept that this world that I and you live in, the rules we follow and the structures we adhere to has been established by people no smarter than you and me. The laws of society and technological developments are not the ongoing work of a divine power; everything has just gradually developed from man's ideas and creations. I would advise you to not accept everything as it appears. Instead, start by asking questions of yourself and your environment. As a small example of this, I was once enjoying an ice-cold can of Fanta Orange on a sunny afternoon. As I looked closely at the can, I noticed that it was owned by the company Coca-Cola. **"That's weird,"** I thought to myself. In my left pocket, I had a packet of Wrigley's chewing gum, so I proceeded to examine the packaging and with this closer inspection, I discovered that the company Wrigley was indeed owned by the Mars corporation.

I started to ask questions and investigate other food brands. This investigation revealed that many of the confectionery and consumer goods available to purchase, such as a packet of M&M's, Skittles,

Wrigley's chewing gum or Hubba Bubba bubble gum, a Galaxy or Snickers bar, Dolmio cooking sauce or even a packet of Uncle Ben's rice will deliver money into precisely the same hands ... that of the Mars corporation. Furthermore, I discovered that the majority of goods that consumers opt to purchase are owned by same ten companies.

There are only a few corporations that control almost everything we purchase—companies like Mars, Coca-Cola, Nestle, Kellogg's, PepsiCo, Unilever, Mondelez, General Mills, Danone and Associated British Foods. It becomes even more intriguing when you realise that some companies own brands that are in direct competition with each other; for example, Volvic and Evian waters are both owned by the same company, Danone. If you required some H2O from your local shop and on sale was a litre bottle of Volvic water for £1.99 and, similarly, a litre bottle of Evian water for £0.99, which one would you buy? This is called framing. Danone has framed the price for a litre of water at around £2, but if you buy the Evian water, you are theoretically saving £1.01. You may even decide to purchase two bottles of Evian water. Either way, the company Danone will receive your money.

Now, I'm not going to start talking about conspiracy theories such as the Bilderberg Group and the New World Order (incidentally, I do find this a very interesting topic of discussion) but I would strongly suggest you attempt to stop fully accepting everything at face value. Information presented to us has many undertones and connotations and it is up to us to filter out fact from fiction. If you have ever witnessed an event first-hand, then later seen or read the news reports on this same event, you will understand how distorted the facts can become ... Why let the truth get in the way of a good story?

Sadly, many of us are not able to question our identity or the environment in which we live. **"Well, that's just the way it is,"** or **"We've always done it this way,"** are two of the most dangerous and defeatist phrases in the English language. It is a weak and rigid mentality that conveys this message to others. Truly great people and leaders will always look for a more logical or economical method of achieving a goal. Admittedly, it's sometimes very hard to do things your own way within a society that is full of moulds and set criteria. I am not asking anyone to stop buying Uncle Ben's rice or packets of peanut M&M's; I merely wish to highlight the need to question information that is presented to us.

One major question that reoccurs at various stages of our lives is, **"What do you want to do when you grow up?"** Or, as you get older, this becomes, **"Where do you see yourself in five or ten years?"** We are all led to believe we must find a role in life to fill; generally, this is as part of a larger company or corporation.

I find it sad that in schools around the world pupils are taught to believe that you can be anyone or do anything that you can dream of. I can vividly remember the first time I encountered and attempted to answer this question. I was a child with a drawing, battling against the age-old dilemma of growing up and chasing a dream and the hard truth of reality. At six years old I handed my teacher a drawing of a brave lion tamer: **"This is what I want to be when I get bigger,"** I stated with resolute determination. He stared at me with a confused look that screamed, **"No chance, son!"** but he opted to smile politely and say, **"I can see you doing that, Peter; in fact, I think you'd be really good."**

Somewhere along our journey towards the real world, we are warned off following our dreams; we sheepishly bury our lion tamer's outfit in a box and place it under the bed. Every year, young adults are sent out into the workplace to become part of a large revolving door of workers filling spaces in companies. It just doesn't add up, does it!? Society sells the dream, an idealistic version of reality, but this sadly only applies to a select few. What is so different or special about this minority of people? Why do they get to fulfil their dreams while the rest of us spend afternoons heating up sausage rolls or sweeping up hair? (Not at the same time, hopefully.) Obviously dreaming of being a brave lion tamer is a bit outrageous, and as we grow, our dreams shape around the world presented to us. Contentment is about finding a happy medium between surviving and thriving in life. Are you living a life with purpose, or do you:

- Feel disconnected or discontent with society and life?
- Dream of achieving something greater than normality?
- Wish to live a full life of memories without a sense of regret?

Many people I have met and spoken with are

floating through life. Sadly, only a select few of these will ever take the necessary steps to eradicate ongoing negative issues. In this book, we will investigate how problems occur and what steps can be taken today to create a positive life change. Though your self-image is not defined by your job, your employment is still a factor that directly affects your happiness. The majority of jobs and positions in companies squash individuality and personality, as most of the aspects of your character will not have a bearing on your ability to successfully complete a task. Why should a company be overly concerned with knowing or understanding the real you!? This creates a society that spends most of its working lives wearing a mask, hiding one's true self and feelings.

Work encompasses the majority of our time on this planet, and during this large chunk of time, we hold back our innermost thoughts and feelings; essentially, we pretend to be happy. I will repeat this: **We are pretending to be happy**! The irony of this predicament is highlighted during the application process. When you apply for a job or a training course, companies will always ask for a personal statement or to complete a section entitled **"Tell us something interesting about you"**. There is minimal long-term worth attached to this particular section of the form for the majority of jobs.

Using an example to put this into context, let's say you apply for a job in a bank. You complete the **"about you"** section in depth; you tell the company all about your travelling experiences and your dreams to play the piano in front of a large audience. You interview well and get the job ... congratulations! After two weeks, you have completed the standardised induction training programme for all new employees and you are now working as a cashier. A customer comes in to change some money into USA dollars and you ask him where he's going and he says, **"New York City." "Brilliant,"** you think to yourself as you have only recently returned from the Big Apple (as mentioned in your "about me" section). You began talking to the customer about places to visit, you mention Central Park, and just as you're about to tell all about your glorious horse-and-carriage ride around the city, you hear a whisper over your left shoulder. **"Move it along."** You turn, embarrassed to see the back of your manager as they walk away.

Employers want an efficient and reliable

workforce and not independent thinkers. Unfortunately, you are just a cog in a larger wheel, which is the sole aim of the employment process—to find someone who fits into the current order of things. Company rules and regulations are emphasised during the induction phase. You are trained to follow a strict protocol and the uniform confirms the final phase of the process, ensuring you are no longer representing yourself and personal life experiences but are a mere talking head for the company. **"We have always done it this way."** You have been inducted to a life of normality and repetition ... I hope for your sake that this is just a pit stop in your race to success and achievement.

The real world is designed to prevent and even punish individuality. We are all wired at a young age to not only judge ourselves but also anyone else who doesn't follow what society has deemed as normal. I will emphasize again that nothing amazing or memorable has ever flourished out of normal. Now, I'm not saying these jobs are bad or insignificant; I am just increasing your awareness of what's really at play here. Indeed, think about the reward structure at some of the major companies. Reward schemes in any form are designed to increase retention of business.

Think about any loyalty card to a store or petrol garage: If you spend X amount of money you will collect X amount of points and eventually you will get X amount of money back. It's an incentive scheme to increase the return flow of repeat business. In the workplace, this idea is replicated to achieve a repeat of what is deemed good behaviour by the management. A particular behaviour, for example **punctuality,** will be highlighted to all other employees within the company. The employee will be singled out and rewarded; other colleagues will then want to show they are able to perform at the level required to also be publicly praised. The result? An increase in positive behaviour and ultimately productivity. Who's the real winner here? Do companies offer a reward labelled "For Just Being Themselves"? If you've ever seen the film *Office Space* (1999), it screams about the pain of normality and a life without drive or purpose. In one scene Jennifer Aniston's character, Joanne, is reprimanded by her boss as he lectures about the fact that the 'flair' (badges) are her opportunity to express herself, and he is not happy that she seems satisfied in only wearing the bare minimum of fifteen pieces. When Joanne's boss once again disciplines her for her lack of badges, she decides that she has had enough and promptly walks out of her job. The reasons for quitting are due to the frustration of poor management and a total lack of freedom regarding decision-making and independence. This is how many of us would act on occasion if we didn't have bills to pay.

I once worked as a gym instructor at a health club that was located in a hotel. I loved this job as I got to work with my friends. We swapped shifts around, exercised on our shifts and, on some hangover days, slept on the massage tables in very dark therapy rooms. Once, the regional general manager for this particular chain of hotels paid us a visit. We were told, **"Make the place as clean as possible and be on top of things when he comes down to the gym in about two hours."** This was a clear message from someone whom we had worked for for over three years, our direct manager. He liked us but knew exactly how lazy we all were in the health club. So with this, we started scrubbing and cleaning all the floors and equipment. We even changed the filters on the swimming pool and the Jacuzzi. The place was looking good … well, better than normal, anyway. We then waited and waited.

Suddenly, the phone rang at the reception desk. **"He's coming now,"** a voice whispered; it was all very cloak-and-dagger. We stood on attention at the reception desk, hands behind our backs, shirts tucked in and name badges on correctly. (Historically, we would swap our name badges around in an attempt to get complaints issued in each other's names.) One of the large glass doors to the health club swung open and in marched four men in suits. We all got introduced to each other and then promptly started a tour of our training facilities. Something very strange happened; me and my mate Dan became extremely professional, almost experts in our field. We talked through the equipment, the number of memberships we had, our roles and why we loved working for the company. I thought to myself, **"Wow, do we actually know what we are talking about!?"** We both tried hard not look at each other because over the smell of bullshit in the air, any eye contact would result in an eruption of laughter. As the tour was coming to an end, we approached the reception area and started to direct the men towards the canteen, then almost in slow motion, the regional manager, Jeff, stopped and looked at me. There was a long awkward pause; Jeff then spoke directly to me. **"Young man, have you** filled out your beard form?" I froze trying not to laugh. I daren't look at Dan. I coughed twice and asked, "Err, what exactly is a beard form?" and he replied, "Have you not heard of a beard form? Well, you have some stubble on your face and if you are planning on growing a beard, the company needs this in writing." Now totally bemused and amused, I retorted "Well, I shaved this morning ... should I complete one every four hours, or just once a day?"

In the corner of my eye, I could now see Dan slowly skulking away with a massive grin on his face, staring intensely at the floor. I could tell he was praying not to burst out with laughter. Jeff came back at me with, "Please don't make fun of our processes, young man; these structures are put in place to keep everyone at this hotel safe." "Oh boy," I thought, "this is escalating very quickly." I had no intention of creating trouble with the powers that be—well, not today, anyway. "Exactly who is in danger from my stubble, sir? I don't plan on attacking anyone with it." He sharply replied, "Don't get smart, young man; if you want a beard, or 'stubble' as you call it, you must complete that form." I responded with the comment that would ultimately lead to me losing one of my favourite jobs of all time. "OK, sir, I will complete the beard form on your request. Shall I grab you a 'thinning hair' form while I'm there? I mean, if you're planning on going bald, I think you should let the company know!" I almost couldn't finish the sentence as I was already laughing, fully aware of what a mischievous comment it was. Dan's laughter echoed loudly inside the male changing room. The four men stormed out, red-faced, with steam puffing out of their ears. I subsequently received my final discipline hearing in that job; one more and I was out, and that did occur for a totally different reason a few months later. Now, what I said and how I behaved was not the correct way to act (I have never responded well to authority), but the point stands. I couldn't even grow a beard in that job without informing the hierarchy. If there isn't any room for stubble, there's no room for individuality … I think that slogan belongs on a T-shirt!

"Ninety percent of adults spend half their waking lives doing things they would rather not be doing at places they would rather not be"
(Why We Work, Barry Schwartz)

This need to fit into a box or a company ideal for eight hours a day takes its toll. Trust me—as well as the gym job mentioned, I have worked at fast-food restaurants, shoe shops and bars. If you are stuck in a job you hate in the short term, you can begin to think about all the positives attached to your job. The first one is maybe that they pay you, you may have colleagues you like and aspects of the job that you find interesting. If you are trapped and frustrated, then it is imperative you find that passion or hobby to fill your evenings and, indeed, your mind. This will be a major factor in being able to remain productive in the workplace. See the bigger picture by installing enjoyment into your days. Discovering a passion or a goal is vital in combating the feelings associated with restraining your true self. A goal will need to be developed so you can focus and work towards it; this will give meaning to your life. After all, a life without meaning or purpose is a life wasted.

To totally counteract this requirement to suppress

your personality, try to find a job where you don't need to—a job where you can be yourself. If you manage to find or even create the job you love, a job that makes a difference or a job that means something to you, then you, my friend, have beaten the system. You are going to spend a large chunk of your life in work. If you are doing something you don't enjoy or something that causes feelings of anxiety, then my advice would be to get out as quick as you can, or at the very least, find a passion. I can't think of anything worse than reflecting on a life without achievement or joy. Too many people work to collect a pension and even count the number of days until they reach retirement. Use the time-travel chapter in this book to assess if you are heading in the direction and the vision of your true self, a vision that may have captivated you as a child ... go become that lion tamer.

The real world and the workplace are full of dreamers who might quit or might apply for a new job or who might go travelling or who might go to the gym or who might not drink this weekend or who might quit smoking ... they never will. Words and empty threats. the world is full of "might" people; they will be working for the same company in thirty years' time, living for the weekend and dreading the Monday morning commute. Once you discover a reason to get up and attack the day, that feeling of anxiety on a Sunday night dissipates. I have been on both sides of the fence and, trust me, waking up on a Monday morning with a sense of purpose is a very good feeling. The "Might" people are not decisive enough to leave their employment in search of a greater destiny. In my experience, these are the same people that spend all day on Facebook and their days off watching TV shows. Just like people counting down to their retirement age, in essence, they are wasting time.

It is a shame that the most valuable entity in our lifetime is not perceived as such; time is undervalued and money is overvalued. Sadly, this realisation often only occurs near the end of a life or after a health scare pertaining to yourself or a family member. I hope that as you progress through these pages, you will begin to appreciate the value of time and a purpose. This may result in small steps away from any individuals with a fixed mindset as you start to find your true self amongst a swamp of normality. The next time someone says to you, **"I might do this,"** turn around and state firmly, **"Go on then … I**

dare you!" I guarantee they will come back with an excuse or a reason they can't travel or haven't read a particular book. I want you to smile to yourself. This person is a "Might"; they do not possess an understanding about the secret codes of life, codes that you are about to discover.

Warm-up task

Do you have a <u>fixed or growth mindset</u>? Select an answer and total the points attached to this response. Be honest with yourself:

<u>*Fixed or Growth Mindset*</u>

<u>**Skills**</u>:   Something you are born with (1 point)

Can be learnt and improved (2 points)

<u>**Challenges**</u>: Are an opportunity to learn and develop (2 points)

Are to be avoided as they will show my failures (1 point)

<u>**Effort:**</u>   Is only necessary when you don't have the ability (1 point)

Is essential in determining success (2 points)

Feedback: I find negative feedback hard to accept (1 point)

I enjoy all feedback as it helps me to improve (2 points)

Mistake: If something goes wrong I tend to blame other people (1 point)

If something goes wrong I use it as motivation to work harder next time (2 points)

Competition: I feel threatened by the success of others (1 point

If others succeed I'm inspired (2 points)

Fixed Mindset: 0–5 points

Mixed Mindset: 5–9 Points

Growth Mindset: 10–12 points

The process of change is possible with dedication and belief. If you scored nine points or less, then this book will help you adapt your thought process and impact all other areas of your life. In essence, together we will be reprogramming your inner dialogue and personal narrator. When faced with a challenge, the person with a fixed mindset responds internally, **"What if I fail? I will be embarrassed."** A person with a growth mindset attaches a different narrative to the same situation: **"I might be able to do this. If I can't, I will one day. I would rather try than not attempt it."**

There are progressive steps you can start to take that will positively influence your life. One such step is to change your internal dialogue and the way you narrate your own life. As we progress through the book, we will take steps towards a better you. Successful living is the creation of small steps completed consistently over time. It has worked for me. I have used the hidden codes found within this book to reprogram my own thought process, become more positive and use these small steps to overcome larger obstacles. Obstacles act as a catalyst for change, forcing development and preparation for all that life has to offer. After all, life is the biggest challenge you will face, but I truly believe all negative experiences make us stronger, culminating in being a big part of the larger steps we take. It's like walking up a flight of stairs—you can't jump to the top without going through the ground level. As you get higher, inch by inch, you forget how high and far you have travelled, and you do not consider past steps, only those which lay in front of you on your path to the top.

We are all products of the adversity created from our environments: single-parent families, adopted, rich or poor. Our environments from an early age shape our character and, depending on the situations we have faced, our resolve and resilience. I consider myself lucky as I had a loving family around me. It was crazy at times, but our house was full of love. However, life wasn't strictly straightforward, I had a mixed upbringing, with my mum looking after me and my sister on her own for a couple of years until she met and married my stepdad.

I can now reflect on these times and how they impacted my life and character, and I can honestly say it all helped me. Adversity forced me to be different; it gave me the desire to move out of home at sixteen to play football, to represent my country at seventeen, and to gain a soccer scholarship in California at the age of eighteen. The resistance I faced as a child made me stronger than others around me; I was more willing to break down moulds and push boundaries. I displayed a dedication to certain areas of my life with a relentless attitude. I don't think I'm more talented than anyone else, but I have fashioned an unwavering work ethic that cannot be beaten. The famous actor Will Smith, who has an interesting and inspiring view of the world, once said:

"The only thing that I see that is distinctly different about me is I'm not afraid to die on a treadmill. I will not be out-worked, period. You might have more talent than me, you might be smarter than me, you might be sexier than me, you might be all of those things you got it on me in nine categories. But if we get on the treadmill together, there's two things: You're getting off first, or I'm going to die." (Will Smith)

When you find a passion in life, this quote will resonate with you. Once you have that passion, the struggle will only emphasise the progress and not the difficulty. If you are going through a struggle (or have come out the other side of one) then I can relate; please trust me when I say it will only serve to make you stronger. The purpose of life is to grow, just like the results of evolution create stronger versions of plants, animals and human beings. If a plant can't obtain water or sunlight, they adapt by leaning towards the sun or, over time, they evolve to be able to store water during barren months so they can survive within their individual environment. For example, cacti are able to survive the harsh desert environment as they have stems that can store water and vast root systems that enable water collection from a greater area; they also have spines instead of leaves to reduce water loss. Adaptations within evolution are the greatest evidence that without a challenge, and the ability to overcome one, there is limited progress or, indeed, survival. Some human beings shy away from things that will help them adapt and refuse to take a risk; we now know that they possess a negative internal voice. Some people act upon the challenges that are forced upon them while others, the best kind, go looking for obstacles to attack head-on ... these people are leaders with a growth mindset, and they evolve to become strong and independent people.

Fundamentally, life is a giant boxing ring. The real world, with its bizarre system structures, becomes your sparring partner. In the ring of life, if you're not jabbing, moving and protecting yourself, then you are getting punched in the face by a big left hand! What happens when you get punched in the face? That's right—you feel pain, and look damaged and aged. You need care and attention, both physical and mental. Psychological support will be required to comfort your ego and reinforce your confidence: **"You are going to be OK; you can return to the ring**

in a few weeks." However, if you stay alert and keep moving forward, you will remain focused and driven. You will return to your corner looking fresh, with a positive self-image, and advice from outsiders will be unrequired. You will remain the captain of your mission, and stopping will only come by way of victory or knockout. For in life, just as in the ring, you will need to be prepared. Prepared for a new challenge or a new beginning, and have a willingness to accept that not everything will always remain the same, and that this is a good thing. Find a purpose and a passion; understand that setbacks will only help you sharpen your focus and resolve. This book will guide you onto a positive pathway to success and happiness, but you and only you will be in charge of the final destination.

When a child or an adult requires advice about their personal life and struggles they may be facing, I often explain the tale of two cyclists. Cyclist A has the best bike, only cycles in the best conditions, and cycles the same route Monday to Friday five days a week with the same group of people. Cyclist B has a pretty old bike; he cycles bumpy and rough roads every day in all conditions, with a variety of different people, for five days a week Monday to Friday. One day a poster goes up in the local town hall: **"Win a trip to Australia, all expenses paid: Meet at White Hill Lane at 7 a.m. on Saturday 23rd October."** "That sounds great," the two cyclists think to themselves. **"I**

would love to go to Australia!" They both wake up on Saturday morning and cycle excitedly to White Hill Lane. When they arrive, there is a long line of identical blue Boris bikes (a very basic bike that you can hire in London for the day) that have been assigned to every contestant. The arrows scattered around White Hill Lane signify that the start of the race is at the base of an enormous hill. A road sign on the grass verge informs all the competitors that the gradient of the hill is 12 percent for a distance of three miles. The cyclists place their helmets on while attempting to get comfy on the rigid seat that rests on the bike's heavy frame. Suddenly a loud crack of thunder erupts from the skies directly above the start line; with this the heavens open, and rain starts to hammer down. My question: Who would be better prepared to attack the large hill and claim the holiday—Cyclist A or Cyclist B? If you had to bet your last £1 or $1 on one of them to win, which one would you select?

All those bumpy and rocky roads in life are there for one reason: to prepare us for that bigger challenge up ahead. The real world will always have a challenge waiting. Self-development and dreams are either stopped by these challenges or, like the cactus plant, you are able to adapt and unearth the mindset and the motivation to overcome them. This book will not only provide you with the tools to adequately prepare, but also to conquer any giant hill that is lurking up ahead.

The secret codes found within these pages are guidelines that will enable you to become realigned with your true self, providing you with a purpose and a passion. Work colleagues, friends and family members will be amazed by the psychological and physiological growth that you experience and display. The following chapters are designed to refresh your reality, adapt your perception and open your mind; I will share many personal stories and experiences that are both lighthearted and sad. Tasks and challenges will enable you to make immediate improvements to your life through the creation of new everyday positive habits.

Ultimately, you are about to discover a proven practical guide for positive self-development and progress across all areas of your life. You will need:

✓   a pen or pencil

✓   A notebook

✓   Self-discipline

✓   Effort

If you have all of the above, then you are ready. Turn the page to start a new chapter...

Name:...

Exam: Life

Time: Unknown

Your time starts now...

Good Luck

New Goal = New Challenges = New You

Or

No Goal = No Change = Same You

Code 1
Learn to Love Negative Experiences

Code 1: Negative experiences such as failure and disappointment are all part of the process to achieving your innermost dreams. It is your ability to remain steadfast and endeavour through these ordeals that will, just like natural selection, create a stronger version of you.

Scenario: John has been offered the opportunity to go on a management training course within his current employment. The course, though notoriously difficult, leads to automatic promotion and there are many financial benefits that are attached to this. However, historically within the company, employees that fail the course at the first attempt dramatically reduce their effort and remain at their current employment level.

Potential outcomes:

A) Go for it and fail, but then opt to play it safe in his current role.

B) Stay where he is, avoiding the embarrassment of failure.

C) Go for it and fail, but obtain further knowledge in the necessary areas and eventually reapply.

D) Go for it and get it.

Progress Means Failure

"If you don't buy a ticket you don't win the raffle!!"
(Old English Proverb)

If you have played football in Great Britain (soccer for our American readers), at some point somebody will have shouted this at you or at somebody on the pitch. Indeed, my mum would tell me this phrase a lot growing up. It became so common that I could sense when she was about to say the phrase, but before she was able to, I would give her a frown and firmly say, **"Give it a rest, woman!"** However, little did I know this would be an overriding default philosophy of mine, subconsciously engrained into my mindset from an early age, and I can't thank my mum enough for this. This little saying provided me with a sense of measured risk-taking that has enabled me to enjoy a varied array of life experiences.

I use the word "measured" because that is how I interpret the statement; it is about winning a raffle, which is a realistic achievement for anyone. It is not referring to winning something against insurmountable odds, like a national lottery; if you haven't won a raffle yourself, I'm sure you will know somebody who has. The raffle, in my eyes, is a realistic and achievable prize. The reward will not be as grand as the million-pound lottery jackpot, but then you can have many attempts at a raffle and the prizes are interesting and varied. The key is, you still need to buy a ticket to win any raffle; essentially, you have to be in it to win it. Just as in life, if you don't buy a ticket, you won't lose any money or effort, but technically you have already lost before the draw has even begun. I would rather lose a thousand raffles with a chance of winning in each one of them than sit there without a hope in hell. This emphasises the difference between a fixed, play-it-safe mindset and a risk-taking growth mindset. I am more than content with living and taking measured risks than I would be playing it cautiously; you only get one run at this life. A growth mindset is willing to take a chance on an idea and fail, rather than failing by standing by and allowing opportunities to pass.

"The trouble with most of us is that we would rather be ruined by praise than saved by criticism"
(<u>Norman Vincent Peale</u>, <u>The Power of Positive Thinking</u>)

The individual with a fixed mindset is afraid of failure and will take criticism negatively. In contrast, the reflective thinkers are the people at the root of all progression; they are self-critical, and this trait enables certain persistence towards a goal or a dream. Think about the young child that only receives positive reinforcement for bad behaviour from a parent too scared to reprimand or set firm boundaries. As this child grows, they will not understand the benefits of failing and getting things wrong.

We cannot pretend to live in a world where we are always correct. Accepting our failures is a crucial step in our self-development; we must understand ourselves in order to progress. If you are unable to evaluate your performance or laugh at your misgivings, then the world is going to be a very tough place for you. You will be forced to wear a mask to hide your faults, and this will only create separation from potential bonds with friends, lovers and maybe even family members. Once you accept yourself, warts and all, the world becomes a much more forgiving place. Having an understanding of oneself will provide a level of self-efficacy that cannot be affected by the day-to-day actions of others; it allows you to step away from some situations and fully commit to others.

Too many people live in the safety net of a comfort zone. Even typing the words "comfort zone" I can feel my toes curl. "Comfort Zoners" go to work, go home, watch TV, sleep, then go back to work. It's a crazy existence, but the fact is, they would rather survive than thrive. This is mere existence and it is purely a fear of failure that holds them back; to me, it is a waste of a life. This type of person is the wealthiest in the graveyard. They will be buried with all of their dreams, hopes, desires and ideas that the world never got to witness because they were too afraid of failure or a negative response. We are all going to end up in the graveyard, but when I go, I want my grave to be worthless. I want to leave this world with a laundry list of achievements and failures. I want people to say, "He put in everything he could into this life; he was a real worker ... never stopped!" Don't take your true dreams with you to the grave. Live a full life, give everything and leave nothing behind.

"It is impossible to live without failing at something unless you live so cautiously that you might as well not have lived at all, in which case you have failed by default."

(J.K Rowling)

Enjoy the Process

I love failure!! I love it; it means many things. It means I am either attempting something I haven't done before or I cannot do or a challenge that I am scared of. It means I am pushing boundaries and living outside of my comfort zone. I challenge you to do something outside your comfort zone at least once a week. Try a handstand, go for a run, paint a picture, complete a Sudoku—anything outside of your norm. Indeed, I spent most of my life too ashamed to attempt a crossword because I felt that I would be unable to complete it and would give up. I now attempt one a week; it took two months before I actually completed one, but if I had not persevered through those failures, it would still remain an uncompleted challenge lurking in my subconscious. Now completed, it clears the pathway for a fresh challenge to be accepted.

In summary, it is better to be failing at a challenge than not attempting one. That is not to say that you are failing in all areas of your life, but it is a good thing to find something to fail at. It means you are progressing towards something, maybe a pathway you have mapped out to a larger long-term goal. Completing a crossword was not nor has it ever been a long-term aspiration of mine, but it was something I wanted to try and it has built into part of a bigger goal, such as writing this book. The challenges overcome along the way to a goal are as important as the goal itself. Now, imagine if someone offered me a manuscript of **"Stop Walking, Start Sprinting"**. I decided to examine the writing and it was good, really good: **"It's yours; you can have it. Just put your name on it and get it published."** Easy. I would be in the exact same position as I am now, but it would have taken a fraction of the time ... Wrong! I would not have experienced the process of writing a book, the research involved and the self-development. I may have achieved a goal, but using shortcuts does not equate to the same feelings. Happiness lies in the journey towards a goal, no matter how difficult it may be. In fact, the greater the difficulty the greater the intrinsic reward. The same analogy can be applied to a physical challenge. Two people aim to reach the summit of Mount Kilimanjaro. One of the climbers has trained for months, researched the process and planned all the minor details that would encompass such a rewarding challenge. They take three gruelling weeks to reach the mountain's peak; the views are glorious and are only visible during the early months of the year. The other person decides to get to the top of the same mountain without training. He arranges a helicopter to take him to the peak of the mountain, where he too soaks up the glorious views from nearly six thousand feet above sea level. They have both achieved an external reward—the view—but only one of them has experienced the self-development that is exclusively linked to the process of accomplishment.

Negative Nigel v. Positive Paul

"He who says he can and he who says he can't are usually both right" *(Confucius)*

In my mind, there's a little voice that appears every time a new challenge is faced. **"You can't do it; you will never do it; you're not good enough."** This voice is a habit of social conditioning. This is basically an echo of what you believe society is going to tell you once you announce your goal to the world, or even to your close friends and family. "This (insert challenge here) is not meant for me; it's meant for other people, better-trained people. People like me and who are from where I'm from can't do this kind of stuff." Well, I am going to tell you something you already know ... you are exactly the kind of person who can achieve the challenge you have set out. Do you know why? Because you have selected it! It is something that interests you, something that ignites passion and, therefore, is meant for you.

If I have learned anything along the way towards some of my challenges that's important to remember, it's that we are all human beings. We are all built very similarly—yes, with some biological differences, but we're very similar in structure. So what is the overriding factor that means somebody can run a marathon while other people can't run for a bus? Hours of training and dedication would be the correct answer, but remember that this all starts with an idea and is supported with a strong belief. An idea originating from the soul and truly believed by the mind is an extremely powerful and unstoppable thing. It is the creation of a purpose supported by positive life habits, such as self-talk, that serves to set humans apart from one another.

Achieving a "Positive Paul" mindset is challenging, if it was easy, everybody would be happy and content. The majority of people are "Negative Nigels" because this takes minimal effort, as faults are easier to find and analyse, both externally and internally. However, once you achieve a positive mindset, nothing can shake it; setbacks are mere speed bumps on your route to success. Negativity will only serve to force you to work extra hard in specific areas, making you even stronger and more prepared for the next challenge. You will slowly start to love life's little speed bumps, perceive them as only challenges to overcome, and utilize them to improve your resolve on the way to becoming a stronger version of yourself. The people that have a growth mindset are able to reflect on performances and methodology and admit their faults in order to progress. Progress is a process and it will not take place overnight.

Fitness and exercise is a way to clearly describe this principle. Let's say you are a 100-metre sprinter and you have a personal best time of 11.9 seconds and you want to get your time down to less than 11 seconds. Those 0.9 seconds will take months of weight training and explosive training. You will have to ensure that you are living the right lifestyle— sacrificing nights out with friends, big family meals and many early mornings. However, even all of this effort will not guarantee that you are able to produce a time under 11 seconds. Still, as long as you believe in the process and do all you can do towards achieving it, you are progressing … and there is a chance. It would be a whole lot easier to not try and explain to people, **"If I really trained, I could do it, but I've lost interest."** That is a fixed negative mindset, one which is scared of failure; one which has an ego. Combined with this fear of failure comes a lack of self-development and, ironically, the biggest risk of all: never knowing or reaching your full potential. What a scary thought, not experiencing failure and therefore never pushing your mind and body to the edge of its capabilities. As in life, competitors will only continue to progress while your own self-development halts.

Andy, a good friend of mine who comes up a couple of times in this book, once said to me, **"I could do it quicker than that."** He was referring to the marathon I had completed the day before! In 2007, my first year out of university, I set myself the challenge of raising money for the charity scope by running the London Marathon. I was very unfit, coming out of four years at university, and I was still drinking heavily at this time. I trained for months, but inevitably I still found the course around London extremely difficult, hitting the famous "wall" at around the nineteen-mile stage. I completed the 26.2-mile course in precisely 3 hours, 51 minutes. I was aiming for under 3 hours, 30 minutes, but by the end I was just delighted to have finished. I arrived at the finish line drained, both physically and mentally. My friends and family looked after me and took me home, where I slept and ate for the day. The elation and buzz of the experience raced through my mind all evening.

The next day I had a lunch with Andy and a few close friends. I replied to his jibe with a smile on my face: **"Well, go do it, then ... apply, mate. I'll look up the website up for you."** I loaded the London Marathon 2008 website up on my phone and starting inputting his data: **"When's your birthday again, mate? And what's your postcode?"** Now the whole table was laughing as he squirmed. He pulled out his planner and said, **"Looking at my schedule, I'm busy for the next ... err, three years!"** We all laughed in unison. Remember, the world is full of these "Might" people who talk about doing something. It's almost as if they believe they can achieve a goal or aspiration to a certain point, but when the reality of the challenge sets in, that internal negative voice increases in volume. Opting to back down, they deflate their ego and return to normality. By the time you finish this book, you will have a focus and a challenge. The negative voice inside your head will not exist, or at the very least, it won't have a say in your progress.

"Our greatest weakness lies in giving up. The most certain way to succeed is always to try just one more time."
– *Thomas Edison*

Negative people see a road bump as a mountain. That challenge is there to break them, to remind them that their chosen purpose is the wrong one. It is not for them; they will never achieve it and they must return back to the drawing board. They are not robust enough to turn negatives into positives; all people with a fixed mindset are unable to do this. They are scared of failure and criticisms; hence, they are static, stagnant in the midst of a moving planet. The very nature of our world is that everything is constantly progressing and adapting. Technology is evolving so rapidly that other devices and companies that do not themselves advance are left behind. I used to use a map to find directions to places I wanted to visit; this was soon replaced by a satellite navigation system, which in turn has now slowly been replaced by maps on phones. Imagine being lost now and asking someone for directions using a map; I think they would be shocked!

These advances have a dramatic effect on other areas of our society, for instance, taxi drivers. "The Knowledge" was a standard test for all drivers and quite an achievement for someone to pass; it involved studying the routes around London or a given area and meant you could qualify to drive around the city.

Fast-forward to the modern era and I press an app button on my phone, a taxi arrives, and the driver requires the postcode of my destination. They're less reliant on human nature and more so on technology. Taxi drivers will have had the option to adapt to these new challenges or to be left behind as their industry advances. If you're not adapting to your environment, unfortunately, you're not thriving.

The mindset behind facing adaptation and new challenges will dramatically affect the outcome. The taxi driver that embraces new ideas and advances to his role will prosper; in contrast, the taxi driver that refuses to change, like in evolution, will not survive. Mindset is everything as we face challenges; to overcome them we must always try one more time. In practice, when I played football if I knew I was going to have a good game the minute something went wrong in a game. If I was playing with a positive mindset, I would misplace a pass and then quickly say to myself, **"Oh well, it's gone now and I'll get the next one right."** If I was low on confidence and misplaced a pass, I would tell myself, **"Oh no, here we go again; that's gone wrong. Everyone thinks I'm not good enough."** You can see it's the same event, but perceived totally differently dependent on the mindset of the individual. Who decides on the way events are perceived? Guess what—we do! It is our internal narrator that translates circumstances into thoughts and, eventually, feelings. Who has control over our internal narrator? You guessed it—we do! Self-talk is a huge part of the process of being able to overcome adversity. If you feel that your self-talk is negative, how can you change this? Just like when I misplaced a pass in football, it can be narrated in one of two ways. Three phrases added onto to any internal negativity can transform the statement into a positive. These are: **"Even the best fail, I will get it right,"** and **"This is temporary; there are better things to come,"** and **"But with practice, I will become better"**. These sentences act as attachments to your thought process. For example:

Negative Narrator	New Positive Attachment
I can't do this	Even the best fail; I will get it right
I am a loser	This is temporary; there are better things to come
I will never be good enough	But with practice, I will become better

Creating a positive inner monologue will start to improve your self-perception. This is a difficult skill to master as we are attempting to change years of habitual behaviour. I have read various methodologies that are aimed at successful reprogramming this negative dialogue:

1) Wear an elastic band on your wrist; every time you negative self-talk, you must stretch the band so it pings you on the skin. The sting of the band will act as a gentle physical reminder that you are mentally hurting yourself.

2) You select a bright object that you refer to every time you are about to engage in negative self-talk or during your negative self-talk; for example, a bunch of bananas. As you start to critique yourself, **"I really messed that..."** you interrupt this analysis by internally saying and picturing **"Bananas!"** You then move on to a new train of thought and away from the original negative thoughts.

3) You are simply able to remember to attach the positive comment onto the negative statement through choice; you are acutely aware when these negative thoughts appear and are equally adept at creating new routines. This starts by acknowledging

the negative thought; for instance, instead of thinking, **"I can't do this today,"** acknowledge this thought by mindfully thinking, **"I notice that I'm having the thought that I won't be able to do this today,"** followed by a positive attachment: **"But with practice, I will become better".** Over time, these positive attachments will become an automatic response.

4) Name your negative thoughts and notice when they appear. As you begin the process of self-doubt or over-critiquing your actions, think to yourself, **"Oh no, here he is, Negative Nigel, moaning away again!"** This will help you to acknowledge, make light of and also separate the negative thoughts from your inner self, creating distance between you and the negative self-talk. This positive shift will help with the completion of challenges and personal goals. If you are able to create a resilience to internalised negative thoughts, then all areas of your life will appear better. The process is like to grey clouds clearing to create a sunny day within your mind.

The mental focus away from negative events, including the over-analytical mind that comes with this, starts to accept failure as a part of a wider learning process. Remember, a positive mind loves a negative experience as it feels a new challenge being established. As mentioned, this is a habitual forming process and, in its infancy, you will be reminding yourself to add the positive attachment, but don't stop as it will slowly become the normal process in which you think. This process can also be externalised; you may find this easier than convincing your internal voice.

Spreading positivity attracts positivity and increased opportunity. When you turn up for work and head over to the coffee pot, who do you speak to and who do you like to avoid? I head to the positive people, the ones who are cheery and ready to attack the day; negativity, especially first thing in the morning, is not what most people are searching for. You may do this subconsciously; it may not even be in person, it may be by email or text, but there will always be someone you feel begrudged communicating with. If you start to verbalise and exude positivity, then people will be more willing to communicate with you. Why? Put simply, it makes them feel good. When somebody asks me, **"How are you today?"** I make a conscious effort of replying, **"I'm fantastic, and you?"** in an enthusiastic manner. I found that there was a period of my life that when anyone asked me how I was, I would respond with **"I'm OK, a bit tired,"** and then the person asking me would reflect these feelings back towards me: **"Yeah, me too; it's been a long week,"** creating a game of negative verbal tennis. What benefit does this have on my day!? I have to do the exact same amount of work and stay awake for exactly the same amount of time and deal with the exact same number of problems. I discovered that by verbally saying I feel great or fantastic, that I actually started to! I managed to trick my mind into forgetting how tired I was and how much work I had to complete that day; my external expressions and interactions started to impact my day positively. I also received increased positivity back; more people would want to interact with me and, therefore, more opportunities would come my way. If you had a spare ticket to an event, who would you consider asking first—the pessimistic person or the positive person? We all want to feel happy and positive; if we radiate this persona outwardly, it will eventually reflect back to us. However, if we become a drain to others' happiness and positivity, then eventually our own source of contentment will dry up or even disappear.

What animal best represents you? This is a question I have been asked in numerous job interviews. I have always believed that there is no correct answer to this dilemma—until recently, that is. Most people believe that a dog is considered man's best friend. How would you describe a dog? What mental images spring to mind? (If you have a fear of dogs, I apologize; maybe skip to the challenge below.) I picture excitement, enthusiasm and a playful spirit. A dog is always happy to see you, always wants to play and has large quantities of energy to burn. In the UK, there have been a string of advertisements that picture cats playing with Frisbees and enjoying games of fetch with the slogan **"Be More Dog"**. I think this saying should apply to many humans out there. The underlying message from these commercials is to be more positive, more enthusiastic and more willing to enjoy the moment. So the next time you are sat in a job interview and are asked, **"What animal best represents you?"** you can now say with a large smile, **"I am a dog"**.

Challenge

Resist the urge to answer negatively to the "How are you?" question. With a smile on your face, respond firmly, "I feel fantastic, and how are you?? Do this with a sense of sincerity and genuine interest in the other person. Feel your mindset change and witness the increased positive interactions and opportunities start to occur. Try this for at least two weeks, especially on Monday mornings!

Superhero 101

> *"Success consists of going from failure to failure*
> *without loss of enthusiasm."*
> *– Winston Churchill*

Indiana Jones was a childhood hero of mine; he lived a life of adventure and intrigue. He had a teaching job at a university and combined this with adventure after adventure. These adventures consisted of a purpose; they all had a focal point. He met adversity on the route to all of these quests, but did he quit? No way! Not Indiana Jones. Quitting was not an option as he was extremely focused on success despite the danger he may meet. What's more, people were drawn to him; they wanted to be part of his journey. Why? Because we all crave a purpose and a challenge, and if we don't have one ourselves, we can see the passion in someone pursuing theirs. Indiana failed and failed, again and again, but he learnt from every failure and every compromising position that he found himself in.

You may not be a fan of Indiana Jones (ouch!), but think about your own favourite superhero or film star. I'm sure they faced adversity to become someone you admire. Films and computer games that involve tough challenges are exciting; they captivate us. Would you pay to watch a film or play a game where nothing made you experience or feel some stress!? In the 1980s, the Rubik's Cube (depending on your age, you may have to Google this) became a craze that swept the nation purely because it was virtually impossible to complete. Indeed, I only managed to complete it once; even this involved carefully peeling off the coloured stickers and swapping them around.

In the 1990s you may remember playing games such as Tetris, Minesweeper, Solitaire or Snakes on your phone or computer; these all offered a mental-based challenge. The graphics or playability of these games cannot compare to that of the modern computer games, but they were enjoyed across the world as they challenged us and we felt a huge urge to persevere with them. The games we played all had a purpose, much like the stars of our favourite films. That purpose enabled us to focus on overcoming the challenge of completing them. Think about your favourite hobby, whether this is a sport, painting or collecting stamps. The greatest sense of achievement lies in completing a difficult task or, in sport, beating a close competitor. You gain a sense of pride and achievement associated with this. I can remember as a young football player enjoying a competitive game against our local rivals. If we won, we would talk about the game all week with smiles on our faces, and if we lost, we would spend months plotting our revenge. On the odd occasion, we would beat a weaker team by ten or twelve goals (no mercy!) but these victories did not bring the same sense of joy; indeed, they would be forgotten about within days. It is the challenge that inspires us. The greater the perceived challenge, then the greater the sense of accomplishment and, therefore, the larger the deposit into our own internal self-esteem bank.

Motivation

Definition: *A reason or reasons for acting or behaving in a particular way.*

If you search through history for the people who have created hugely successful lives, the majority of them will have suffered some form of setback. Many of these stories are well documented, such as J.K. Rowling, Michael Jordan or Steve Jobs. J.K. Rowling created the Harry Potter series, one of the most successful book and film franchises of all time, from a coffee shop while receiving welfare. As a single parent, she was struggling to support her young daughter while chasing her vision. Michael Jordan became the greatest basketball player of all time after not being selected for his high school side. In 1978, Michael failed to make the varsity team as a sophomore at Laney High School in Wilmington, North Carolina. Steve Jobs dropped out of university and created Apple computers from his parents' garage. He subsequently got sacked from his post as director after the board lost faith in him. He then founded NeXT Computers, a company that would take control of Pixar. This animation company introduced itself to the world with *Toy Story* and has gone on to make some of the all-time classic animated films such as *A Bug's Life*, *The Incredibles* and *Up*. Steve Jobs was rehired in 1996 by Apple to return as CEO. Some people embrace adversity while others allow it to destroy them.

What drives people to succeed when all the odds are stacked against them? How did J.K. Rowling keep writing in the face of such huge adversity? Yes, having a clear vision of what you want to achieve is crucial, but without motivation, there is zero chance of success. Motivation is a key ingredient in life; it is essential in overcoming obstacles and dealing with negative experiences. Motivation will generally be far greater if you are doing a job or completing a challenge you enjoy and if you have an end goal or long-term plan associated with these. Achieving a goal signals the release of dopamine within the brain. Dopamine, the feel-good chemical, is linked to motivation and achievement. We will examine this chemical, in combination with other neurotransmitters, in greater detail in the next chapter. Momentarily, let's accept that passion and motivation are exclusively connected, and you will not be able to sustain the endeavour necessary to obtain a long-term aspiration without both of them. Passion without motivation becomes laziness, and likewise, motivation without passion turns into boredom and a lack of creativity. Both are needed in order to be truly successful. Hence, it is important to find a passion that focuses your life on something that you believe in. If you decide on the direction of your life, then the motivation should be relatively easy to find. Motivation can be lost if you repeatedly fail and start to decide you are not able to complete the vision that originally inspired you. A positive growth mindset is important to learn from lessons along the way, but how can we maintain motivation even when we have a found a passion?

Motivation separates code followers from the rest of society; after all, you have had the motivation to look for answers, to change aspects of your life and to start your journey by purchasing this book. **"What's the easy option? Anybody could do that right now."** This is a phrase I use when my motivation is lacking, especially on early morning workouts or after a long day at work. Usually, the answer to the question is a lazy one, such as, **"Stay in bed,"** or **"Eat some fast**

food". Like I said, the easy option. It is easy to be unmotivated, it is easy to quit and it is easy to not care. Sometimes being motivated means doing the hardest thing. Easy options are not there to challenge and shape us; they are a safety net for those of us who are not prepared or ready to become a stronger version of ourselves. Remember, taking the hardest option also provides a sense of reward that taking the easy option simply does not provide.

Motivation creates a snowball effect in all areas of your life; its benefits will be evident both in your home life and your working life. A positive cycle is developed when motivation leads to achievement, which in turn generates an increase in motivation levels. It is important to set smaller attainable goals within the framework of your long-term target to keep motivation levels at an optimum level. For example, if you set yourself the target of playing basketball for the Los Angeles Lakers, then without sub-targets, you would awaken each day with a sense of disappointment. **"I am not an LA Laker yet; when's this going to happen!?"** Eventually, a pattern of negativity and a lack of motivation will start to be established, despite you being totally passionate about this dream. However, if we framed this target differently, we could maintain the motivation required to achieve this goal:

Goal: To Play Professional Basketball

This Year: I want to make my high school team and start every game

How: I need to work on my jump shot and improve my fitness

Jump Shot - Mondays /Tuesdays & Thursdays – work on technique, complete skill challenge at the end of session and record results to see progress.

Aim 1 – to achieve 10/10 successful jump shots by the end of August Y/N

Fitness – Wednesday & Sunday – Hill run timed and results recorded. Increased explosive work on legs; vertical jump recorded once a month.

Aim 2 – To increase my vertical jump by 2.5 cm by the middle of August Y/N

The goal of playing for the LA Lakers remains in place; it has simply been broken down into manageable chunks. Remember, progress is the completion of small steps repeated consistently. The goal is now time-based and target orientated; i.e.

complete the jump-shot challenge and improve vertical jump by the middle and the end of August. If these smaller components aren't achievable, then they can be broken down even further and re-established; if they are achieved, then we can plan to set new targets that build on our accomplishments. The bonus is that by achieving these smaller targets, like ticking off mundane jobs on a to-do list, it feels good while representing progress, which in turn fuels the motivation necessary for the passion. As we achieve or fail at goals, we can reflect on and assess our progress. The pathway to your long-term goal may only become truly clear as you start to check off smaller, bite-sized goals on the journey. Having written evidence of completed targets as to-do lists serves as a reminder of how far you have come; it's a useful tool for reflective thinkers. Remember that one challenge you thought that you wouldn't be able to do or that skill that took you forever to understand? Well, guess what ... you did it, and you have the proof. Furthermore Dopamine, the reward chemical, is released within the brain as progress occurs and this, in turn, creates a motivation boost. Oh, the mighty power of a checklist!

What does motivation look like? It looks like early

mornings and late nights. Waking up before the alarm and working on goals while others sleep. It means fitting time around work and your social life to keep trying new challenges. It is about being productive 24/7. Time is precious and is not to be wasted; **"I'm just killing time"** is not a phrase in my vocabulary. The feeling of completing challenges increases our motivation; targets need to be attainable as the quicker we can tick them off, the better. It is about being relentless in the pursuit of something bigger. Quitting is not an option. Adaptation, yes; breaking down goals into attainable targets, yes; but quitting, no.

Extrinsic motivation means that your desire to achieve is driven by external resources. You may want to achieve that promotion at work to increase your income or impress family and friends. In a sporting context, it would be similar to entering a tennis tournament to win the prize money that is attached to the final game. The chances of disappointment are increased as there can only be one winner and even then, the victory is a tangible object. We use motivation to achieve goals, but do all of these goals make us happy? Extrinsic items have a temporary sense of pleasure attached to them; there is always something more for us to chase or try to collect. Think about that latest pair of jeans or that phone you just had to have; maybe it even forged a deep desire within you to possess it. Now fast-forward three years. Will you still have the same feelings towards these items? No, the instant gratification from new items wears off over time; they will not provide you with lifelong happiness. They are just white noise that hides the desires of your true self. Sadly, some people will spend their entire lives buried by this white noise and thus will be unable to stop and concentrate on what really matters.

Have you ever watched a kid at Christmas rip through present after present without taking a moment to appreciate the gifts? They are experiencing the instant gratification that comes with material things. Some people mask emotional voids with possessions; this is not a route to happiness, but merely a way of hiding from it. What do you remember from your childhood? I remember trips away and visits to interesting places; I remember winning sporting events and spending time with my family. Of course, the odd toy has been stained in my mind's eye, but even the toys I remember are only fondly thought of because of the fun I had with them or because of who had gone to the effort to buy that new toy I so desperately desired.

Indeed, only a few rare possessions hold sentimental value. If your house was on fire, what would you want to save? I'm guessing mostly personal possessions, items that are irreplaceable. Just like intrinsic motivation, these items hold an internal value to you. If your goal stems from an inner desire or a need to fulfil a particular challenge, it will, in my experience, be a greater motivational tool than any tangible or monetary value. One of the aims of this book is to help you to add intrinsic value to your life. Some of the smaller goals I have set in the past have been to read a book a week, contact a family member every day and spend five minutes a day reflecting on the positive moments. These are all internal goals for me; they are helping my self-development and self-efficacy, and there is not an external reward for phoning my mum. I do this because I love her, it makes us both feel more connected and it makes me feel more positive.

I want you to set three possible goals you could work towards. Don't be afraid or embarrassed to dream big. If your dreams and desires don't scare you, then they are not grand enough. We will refer to these in later chapters. The goals can be related to work, personal life or both. Communicate with friends and family and take the time to decide and plan and what will be involved. I.e. Goal: Learning a new language. Process: Researching foreign languages; visiting the library; buying a CD. Searching for nearby classes; planning a trip abroad.

Task 1: Goal-Setting

Goal	Process Will Involve
1.	
2.	
3.	

Planning for long-term goals is a very important process in your self-development. In the example of learning a new language above, I could feel a sense of excitement at the thought of achieving the smaller steps linked to the challenge, followed by being able to put all these skills into practice on a holiday. It is crucial to visualize the goal, the process and the final outcome. Remember, smaller steps build the foundation for a greater challenge. If you have listed three goals, then congratulations, you have started your journey to becoming a better and stronger version of yourself. Setting goals is an essential part of your toolkit; this will enable progress to both occur and be measured.

Lesson: A negative thinker focuses on the challenge in every opportunity; a positive thinker focuses on the opportunity in every challenge. History proves that those people who are challenged in life and face failure head-on are more likely to experience success. Sometimes you have to hit rock bottom to reassess your life, redefine who you are and establish new goals. Start again with a new foundation and belief system; this may begin with your inner dialogue. Rebuild your life on principles that you feel are most important. In summary, go out and fail. Fail every day; fail as much as you can. If you are failing with maximum effort, you are progressing, moving forward and becoming a stronger version of you.

Key Words:

Goals * Challenges * Growth * Focus * Effort * Intrinsic * Fantastic

Be Better Than You Were Yesterday...

Code 2
Meet Your New Drug Dealers:
Laughter & Exercise

Code 2: Laughter & Exercise – Visit these two characters as often as you can. Being a physically stronger version of yourself will impact all areas of your life, including the ability to sleep, learn and focus, while laughter will keep you in the present moment.

Scenario: Bob hasn't exercised for years. He feels unhappy and overweight. He has given up on the idea of having an athletic physique and feels ashamed of his current state of health. One of Bob's colleagues is arranging a staff rugby match against a rival company. He has asked Bob to play.

Potential Outcome:

A) Feeling overly self-conscious, Bob decides not play; there is no change to his circumstances.

B) Bob plays and he enjoys it. He starts to look into attending local rugby clubs.

C) Bob plays but he doesn't enjoy it; he now understands that rugby is not for him.

D) Bob plays and enjoys the experience. He has started to build relationships with other staff members.

Activate the Mind

The best drug dealers you will ever meet are called laughter and exercise. Both of these characters are going to positively transform your life. (This will be the only time I recommend experimenting with chemicals!) These two popular characters can occasionally be very tough to pin down, but they are happy to deal their chemicals to people of all ages, races and sex. Laughter is definitely a tough nut to crack; he can be found in the lightest but also the darkest of places. Your mind will often attempt to fight against his wicked spell, but eventually, I hope you are able to admit defeat to his devilish nature. Once you have spent some moments with him, you cannot help but be hooked by the feelings created. Furthermore, I guarantee that all the times that you fully submerge yourself in his company will be etched in your memories forever. If real-life situations don't enable the two of you to meet and, therefore, the chemical release to occur, then outside stimuli such as films, books or even attending stand-up comedy may assist. We all have a natural affinity to laughter; he is captivating and the glue that bonds many friendships. Think back to the last time you laughed so hard it hurt and your eyes watered with joy. How did you feel afterwards?

Likewise, exercise is a cruel mistress. Similar to laughter, you can become addicted to the feelings she creates. She requires a bit more commitment than laughter, especially regarding meeting times and locations. There will be days when she is difficult to find; sometimes you just haven't got the effort to put into meeting after a hard day's work. Planning to meet up with exercise and failing to do so can be frustrating and provide you feelings of disappointment and despair. However, as long as you keep putting in the effort and stay focused, then you will get to meet her. If you are able to find a common interest, then you will become good friends. Exercise will allow you to experience the glorious rush of pain-relieving and feel-good chemicals; the more frequently you visit, the more you will enjoy all the benefits until the process becomes habitual. The forming of exercise and laughter as habits will create a huge life shift in the direction of positive change. The currencies both these two scrupulous characters deal in are called neurotransmitters namely endorphins, oxytocin, dopamine and serotonin.

Quick Science Lesson – Today's Focus: Biology

❖ Endorphins are produced by the body and act to reduce pain—hence, the name endorphin (a shortened version of morphine). Endorphins interact with the receptors in your brain that reduce the perception of pain, triggering a positive feeling in the body.

❖ Oxytocin is a 'Bonding" hormone which helps you to build trust relationships with people. Humour supports its release and you are more likely to bond with people who make you laugh.

❖ Dopamine creates the desire to repeat a certain behaviour or act; it is involved in all addictions. It is the chemical that creates motivation.

❖ Serotonin makes you feel of worth and importance. Low levels of this chemical cause depression. Studies have shown that an improved diet, exposure to sunlight and regular physical activity will facilitate an increase in serotonin levels.

❖ The body releases these chemicals during exercise and laughter.

The best advice I can give anyone who is questioning their place in this world, unsure of their purpose and feeling unhappy with life, is to **get outside and get active now!** If you are not an active person, then I cannot stress strongly enough the importance of exercise and physical activity—not just exercise, but importantly, outdoor exercise. Exercise outside in open spaces will be the key to positive progress and a notable starting point for many readers. Becoming active improves the productivity and overall efficiency of your body. Aesthetically, you will start to notice changes that will, in turn, improve your self-esteem. In addition, exercising outside, especially where there are large open green spaces and views, increases one's belief that we are all part of something greater than ourselves. The environment has elements that engage the senses, as it may be raining, windy, sunny or snowing, all adding to the sensations being stimulated and the reward of the challenge. If you are feeling a bit low or down on your luck, then stop reading and put this book down, get your trainers on and go for either a walk or a run. What are you waiting for? Go!

Challenge

Physical Education

Today I (Insert Name) ....

ran/walked for...**minutes.**

OK, I hope you're back from your run or walk and you feel positive. Those chemicals are all yours ... enjoy! Of course, in stark contrast, you may not have moved from your current location, tut tut! If you ran or walked, then how you do feel? I would put my mortgage on you feeling better than you did previously. But why? You feel better because of the physical benefit of exercise: the increased blood flow around your body but primarily due to the release of dopamine, serotonin and endorphins the natural feel-good chemicals. Fundamentally, you squashed that negative voice in your head and you are currently experiencing a sense of achievement and pride. Imagine doing that five times a week and becoming stronger and healthier each time!

Or, if you're in the second group of readers who listened to the negative voice, who doubted themselves, who maybe have a fixed mindset … how do you feel? I'm guessing the same or worse. You have surrendered from a challenge and it has negatively impacted your self-esteem and view of self-worth. You have stayed in your comfort zone, worried about a challenge that you might not be able to succeed at. Well, guess what—that's exactly the point of any challenge. If you succeeded in every physical challenge set before you, then these challenges have all been the equivalent of opening a can of beans or you are Superman or Superwoman.

It's good to have something challenging in your path, especially something of a physical nature, as any resistance produces results. Walk into any gym in the world and you will see a long line of "resistance machines. Why? Because resistance forces a response from the body. With regards to physical activity, this resistance starts in the mind before it has a chance to hit your body. Once you have found a challenge, you must be motivated towards completing it. The challenge could be a charity fun run, a road cycle race up a large hill or a five-km swim, but whatever it is, you will need to address the mental and physical resistance associated with it. To make changes and become a stronger version of yourself, you must break through barriers for progression to occur. In all aspects of life, from what I have witnessed, resistance is the key to progress, both physically and mentally.

"Exercise is as effective as certain medications for treating anxiety and depression."
(John J. Ratey, Spark: The Revolutionary New Science of Exercise and the Brain*)*

The benefits of physical exercise are well documented. As part of your personal growth and self-development, this is going to be an essential process. As well as the aesthetically pleasing results of pushing your body into a new shape through increased muscular and cardiovascular resistance, there are the psychological benefits. As explained, it is during exercise that you will receive your fresh hit of pain-relieving chemicals called endorphins, reward chemicals called dopamine and an increased sense of self-worth by raising serotonin levels. I believe these feel-good chemicals are enhanced when you achieve something that was originally perceived to be high in difficulty, forcing you to contemplate quitting, just not committing the act of giving up. Physical activity can reduce your risk of developing <u>depression</u> and <u>dementia</u>; it will also help to treat depression if you already have this condition. Trust me when I tell you that being active will make you feel happier as you gain an improved self-image. Introducing a regular exercise pattern into your daily routine will also aid sleeping if this is an issue for you, as it has been with me in the past. I have spent many a frustrating night not being able to relax and settle into a deep sleep, but as soon as I started pushing physical boundaries and increasing my serotonin levels, this all changed.

"We sometimes lose sight of the fact that the mind, brain, and body all influence one another. In addition to feeling good when you exercise, you feel good about yourself,"
(*John J. Ratey*, <u>Spark: The Revolutionary New Science of Exercise and the Brain</u>)

So there are drugs out there that we all have access to, ones that will make us feel happier and sleep better, and the side effects of these drugs include an increase in focus and productivity with a better physical appearance. The payment for this drug (the feel good chemicals) is a combination of time, effort, dedication and the chemical hormone cortisol. Cortisol is produced by the adrenal gland during stressful situations. In a stressful situation, your body activates the "fight or flight" response. This is your biological response to stress. Prolonged stressful situations keep cortisol levels high within the brain. This can result in depression and anxiety. Laughter and exercise will provide you with the chemical's you require to make you happy and content while also reducing one that creates stress, sounds like a good deal to me. I think you would agree that being active is the single best thing you can do to make yourself feel better right now, and the best thing about these amazing drugs is that they are all free, readily available and you can self-prescribe this wonderful remedy.

The primary neurotransmitter that is associated with exercise is the chemical endorphin. However, dopamine has also been shown to be strongly linked with exercise and highly motivated individuals. Dopamine, like endorphin, is a neurotransmitter but it creates a feeling of reward, achievement and self-accomplishment. Creating and completing intrinsically set goals for ourselves will allow this chemical to action within the brain, especially as we feel progress towards a vision that we have established. Oh, the mighty power of a checklist strikes again! Dopamine is highly involved in the creation of motivation as we enjoy this feeling of reward and want to experience it again. The dopamine pathways within our brains are unique from person to person, as we progress through life we each receive dopamine hits from various sources this may be food, exercise, playing a computer game or even social media. Unfortunately, some people also receive their dopamine hits from drugs such as alcohol, nicotine or even gambling. This neurotransmitter establishes a strong need to recreate any stimuli that will enable its release. The good news is we can, over time, retrain this neural pathway, and in a solution focused approach, opt to replace negative behaviours with positive ones. As explained, exercise provides that dopamine release especially as we work towards a goal. Unfortunately, receiving likes or comments on social media is a far easier and quicker way for most people to receive their dopamine hit, yet this is ultimately unfulfilling. In summary, dopamine creates the desire to repeat a certain behaviour or act and it is involved in all addictions. Take a second to think about what makes you feel good or what actions you rely on daily, these acts are creating a dopamine release within your brain. Focus on the negative ones and start to think about how you can replace them with positive life experiences, include this process in your long term plan or goals.

Remember, being active is the difficult option; staying in bed or not going the gym is the easy option. Therefore, we will need the motivation to ensure that we are able to start being and remaining physically active. We have examined the value of setting life goals. Maybe one of your goals already consists of a physical challenge; if this is not the case, it may be worth including one. For example, being able to complete ten push-ups or a one-mile run and then slowly working towards this target while keeping track of your progress. Imagine if, alongside this challenge, you decided that you wanted to eat healthier and focus on your dietary intake; suddenly the progress effect is snowballing and we are becoming a stronger version of ourselves—and enjoying it.

Make no mistake—the impact of these changes will be witnessed at your place of work and, more importantly, with your friends and family. When you are active and feeling good, you carry a quiet confidence and directness that others are drawn to and attracted to. I know, as I have been at both sides of the coin. I previously mentioned my back injury in 2014. As part of the recovery, I started walking—and I mean I walked and walked and walked. One day, while walking, I discovered a pull-up bar in my local park; little did I know that this single discovery would transform my whole life. I completed one pull-up—yes, one pull-up—and it was a struggle. I vowed there and then that within one month I would be able to do ten pull-ups. One month later I achieved this personal target, elevating my confidence and self-esteem. Slowly, pull-ups became an obsession of mine. I discovered on YouTube various moves and skills that I could learn and self-teach. The activities and skills I developed all related to the term "calisthenics", which means body-weight exercise. By chance or by destiny, I had found a new purpose that was driving me towards something bigger. I am still training and feeling good every day; I think it's a combination of working out outdoors and enjoying the process of the progress. I have since developed a website, www.UrbanCalisthenics.com, where others can learn more about the sport including how and where to get started, while being able to interact with contributors and athletes from all around the world.

I encourage you to try to find a form of physical activity that you enjoy. If you are able to find something you find fun and that keeps you active, it's win-win. This could be anything from ice skating to rock climbing to cycling to walking to bowling or any of the array of sporting options out there. The options and access to sports facilities are vast; I'm sorry, but there is no excuse. Additionally, as with the exercise I chose to follow, there is no cost involved in many forms of physical activity; it's just a matter of making a decision and fully committing to it. You may even find people that share a similar interest as yourself at some of these activities or groups you attend; this could potentially open up a whole new social circle to you. A sport that you enjoy is something that will give you purpose and energy your whole life, so if you haven't found it yet, keep looking; it's out there waiting for you.

I recently completed a "Tough Mudder" run; it was an incredible experience. The run consisted of twelve miles with a variety of obstacles on the route, including ice baths, a tear gas tunnel and a barbed wire army crawl. When the race started, the host asked the competitors if anyone had completed a "Tough Mudder" run before; as hands raised towards the sky, it was apparent that some competitors had completed over ten runs. The event created a real community spirit and provided athletes with an event that you could focus on and train for each year. The race is not timed as it is about teamwork and overcoming challenges as part of a wider community. Sport, like laughter, is the glue that bonds friendships; it is the glue that bonds many communities and groups. If you walk down to your local park you will see dog walkers, runners, maybe some circuit-training classes and some bowls taking place. Take a closer look at the bowls game and, in particular, the age of the competitors. Do you think they have played this game their whole lives? Has it been a long-standing or underlying desire? The answer to both is no. However, these people have found a common interest that their ability allows them to enjoy and also receive the physical and mental benefits from. I know when I retire I will definitely take up the game; I have played bowls on holidays in the past and I can see the appeal. Age, location and finances do not affect your ability to be active and healthy; it could be to run a marathon, climb Kilimanjaro or to be able to do ten pull-ups. Set yourself a personal challenge and commit it to it. To really make a leap forward in your development, combine this with raising money for a charity.

In our scenario, "Bob" had the opportunity to compete in a team sport. Team sports are a huge bonus to anybody's life. The social benefits of competing with other people and experiencing the highs and lows that are associated with this cannot be replaced in the workplace or elsewhere in society. I have been fortunate enough to play football at a high level with some of my best friends. We have created fun memories from training together every day, going through tough periods as a unit and also winning competitions together. At university, as part of the football team, we would have to attend gym sessions at 7 a.m. on a Monday and a Friday morning. As you can imagine, the weekends were pretty manic after a win or loss from the football match played on a Saturday, as we all eagerly spent any money we had received from our respective clubs for playing that day. However, there was something about those 7 a.m. gym sessions on a freezing cold December morning that brought us all together. I used to secretly love them.

We would arrive in the gym and it would be empty. Once the music had started playing, I could feel the energy flowing around my body and mind, and I would begin winding everybody up, making sure I talked to everyone at some stage during the training session. Incidentally, I also worked my socks off and most of the time I would be the first to arrive and the last to leave. Mentally and physically I would feel amazing all day after that gym session; maybe even back then I realised the benefits of exercise and socialising. Indeed, I now understand that the chemical release of oxytocin during team training sessions increased my positivity. Oxytocin is the chemical that is involved in bonding and making you feel part of something, humour and sharing time with similar people increases its release. Therefore, there are definitely some extra benefits from playing a team sport. I will never forget the feeling of one of my best friends scoring a winning goal or saving a penalty; the love and euphoria that you experience in that single moment is indescribable. Even without the competitive element in sport, the social aspect of any team sport remains a positive factor in life. This may be having fun at a training session or a drink in the bar after a game. If you can find a sport that you can share with other people, the benefits will transcend the game, spilling into your life.

Another positive influence of sport is the structure it will give to your life. For years I have trained on Tuesday and Thursday nights and played football on Saturdays; this structure ensures I have some forward planning and focus. This is a good thing. Exchange watching TV or wasting time on a computer game for training, and you will start to see the huge swing in the right direction that a structured approach to exercising offers.

When I trained with my friends, I enjoyed every training session, every coach journey, every hotel we stayed in and, as mentioned, every gym session. I laughed and smiled a lot with my teammates, obviously; I was doing something I enjoyed. However, I discovered that smiling at people and laughing with people is reciprocal. Just like positivity, the more you put out there, the more you get back. It's like the universe wants us to smile and laugh. Feelings of being part of something bigger and enjoyable develop once you start to share laughter and new experiences with friends. The feeling of playing a sport with friends, and working hard while receiving all the psychological benefits linked with this process equals feeling good!

Laughing is an exercise for the soul, and you *must* do it at every opportunity. As you get older, you'll laugh less and less; some people will even fight against laughing, but the ones that laugh and smile will remain young at heart. Unfortunately, many adults lose the ability to laugh—not the physical ability, but the conscious decision to allow happiness to be displayed so readily. It stems from internal negativity and the perceived worries and stressors in their lives. Laughing would be deemed inappropriate. As adults we have very challenging jobs; children and young adults won't understand that we haven't got time to be happy. These adults are afraid to visually display happiness, yet if called upon they will be able to fake a laugh to be socially polite, especially inside the workplace. Ironically, if their boss or a potential customer made a joke, then these people would be the first to belly laugh, the mask-wearers. Take that mask off, smile and enjoy laughing—not to be polite, but because you have found pleasure in the present moment.

Control Your Duck

'Ducklings follow the mother Duck like emotions follow your thoughts, the two are closely connected'

Laughing as many times a day as you can decreases stress and anxiety and also triggers the release of endorphins, the body's natural feel-good chemicals. How do you consistently get hold of these amazing chemicals? By exercising and laughing a lot. Easy, right!? Laughing literally makes you feel better; it's scientifically proven. So why not do it more? If only it were that easy. First, we need to find out what makes us laugh, and then we need to be in the mood to laugh. **"I'm not in the mood"** is a common phrase in England. Ironically, the funny thing about moods is that they are dictated by our own internal thoughts—thoughts that are under your control, or, at least, the ones you choose to deeply investigate and analyse are.

As we have discussed in previous chapters, if you think positive, you will feel positive. Let me repeat that: If you think positive, you will feel positive! Yes, it's that straight-forward. Too often people get caught up in a cycle of focusing on negative thoughts and over-analysing these thoughts until they start spiralling into a dark place of self-pity and hate. Hopefully you are starting to add a positive attachment to your internal thoughts and are externally displaying positivity. Your duck represents your thoughts, and the ducklings that follow the duck are your feelings. The two are intertwined and connected. Once you understand this concept, you realize the irrelevant and harmful nature of thinking anything other than positive thoughts. There is nothing better than thinking positively; by doing so you are able to create a barrier between yourself and negativity, and behind this barrier, nothing can affect you. It's a positive bubble that surrounds you and any negativity bounces off. It will protect you against issues, like the robots within society, that may ruin somebody else's day. It allows a certain amount of resilience against anything that goes wrong. Things go wrong for everybody, every day, but the resilience established with a positive bubble will act as a shield, warding off negativity. However, if you are feeling negative and you have not yet managed to add positive attachments to your inner dialogue, then smiling and laughing could be the catalyst to set you free. Laughing just once or twice a day could be enough to start to bring increased enjoyment into your life. Allow yourself the opportunity to laugh; guide your duck onto the side of laughter over anger. Laughter, like exercise, can create a snowball effect in your life once you decide to open the door to it.

Task 2: Fun Times

Make a list of three situations where you can remember laughing so much it hurt or brought tears of joy to your eyes. This can be from any time in your life: a standout school memory, a moment on a holiday or even your favourite scene in a film.

Funny Memories	People Involved
1.	
2.	
3.	

These situations are important; they are cemented in your memory because of how they made you feel at the time. As I start to recall my own personal memories I can't help but smile and laugh. Though I am thinking about school friends that I have not seen in over ten years, I will always share these memories with them even as we age and new memories are created. Memories that involve laughter stay with us forever. Reliving happier times or moments can provide your brain with a boost of the feel-good chemical serotonin. The ability to mindfully reminisce about happier times is called 'state-dependent recall'. This process transports your emotions back to the time when a particular memory was created, in essence reliving past positive experiences to once again feel positive in the present moment. Do not move on from this task until you have completed it (remember, you promised!), even if it takes a few days to recall such instances. You may have to email or call old school friends or work colleagues to jog your memory.

"A day without Laughter is a Day Wasted"
(Charlie Chaplin)

I can remember being in Year 7 at secondary school and queuing up for some hot food at lunchtime. I loved school dinners; I only ate sandwiches for all of my time in primary school so I looked at hot food as a treat now that I was attending

"Big School". As I queued with my friend Ian, I noticed the button on my school trousers was hanging by a thread; these were trousers from my primary school days so they were already a little snug. As we shuffled forward in the dinner line I felt my trousers start to slip below my waistline. I quickly grabbed them above the zipper, **"Oh great,"** I **thought** as I held my trousers up in the middle of the packed lunch hall. I grasped them tightly as we got nearer to the front of the lunch line. Ian started telling me about a TV show that he had watched the night before. Around this time in England, we had a famous TV presenter called Bruce Forsyth; he was the host of many quiz shows throughout my teens and twenties. Ian decided to re-enact one of his poses: a sideways stance with the right hand punching the air while the left arm extended backwards. Bruce Forsyth would enter the stage with his catchphrase: **"Nice to see you, to see you ... Nice!"** as the crowd cheered he would then strike this very pose. However, as Ian raised his right fist in the air, he knocked a plate of food (which I think was roast beef) out of a passing Year 11's hand. The plate twisted and spun in the air until, in a flash, it crashed to the floor, landing in pieces at our feet. Now, anybody who has experienced canteen life in England will know the response from the rest of the hall was not one of sympathy; what followed was one giant round of applause superseded by a round of cheering and wolf-whistling. In fairness to the Year 11, who had recently lost his dinner, he started to laugh. A poor old dinner lady came across to help clean up the mess. Ian was in shock and I could see him welling up as the very scary Mr Bennet slowly approached us both: **"What on earth have you two been doing here!"** he bellowed at us. Ian froze as a tear ran down his cheek; it was then that I realised I would have to explain the situation.

"It was an accident, sir," I said nervously. Mr Bennet, who was roughly six-foot-three-inches tall with a scruffy dark brown beard, replied as all teachers do: **"Well ... I'm waiting for an answer."** So I began to explain about Bruce Forsyth and his new pose and how Ian was trying to show me. **"New pose? I don't believe you."** Mr Bennet continued, **"Show me, boy!"** I slowly and very nervously looked at him. I then looked at Ian and then at the Year 11, who was still smiling. **"Well, he goes like this, sir."** I turned side on and extended my left hand behind me and punched the air with my right hand, creating a perfect demonstration.

Well, almost perfect. As I recreated the scene, another Year 7, Tommy, was walking past with his empty plate, and I subsequently knocked this out of his hand. **"Oh, my God,"** Ian said aloud over my left shoulder as the plate, along with the knife and fork, spun and twisted in the air, in what felt like slow motion, until everything crashed onto the hard canteen floor. The hall yet again was very sympathetic as it erupted with loud laughter in unison, but the onlooking crowd's response felt far more intense this time. I looked at Ian once again and he was still red-eyed, but now he too had a large smile on his face. The Year 11 from the first plate incident was also laughing and Mr Bennet, well, he was still angry: **"Pull your trousers up, boy, and go to my office!"** Yep ... sure enough, as the events unfolded in front of pretty much the whole school, my now-unfastened trousers had slipped to the ground and they were now resting comfortably around my ankles, revealing my brightly coloured green boxer shorts. It was a truly glorious moment for Ian, my school mates and the rest of the student body, but not so much for myself.

I still recall this story with Ian when I see him or speak to him on the phone. We were only eleven years old at the time, but it still makes us laugh to the present day.

Lesson: Laughter and exercise are good for the mind, body and spirit. Being physically active is a major step towards a positive and progressive life. The type of activity can be anything from walking to ironman competitions, but having a good level of physical fitness impacts all other areas of your life. If you perceive that you look good and are achieving personal fitness goals, then you will feel good. Exercise also helps with the ability to focus, learn and sleep. Laughter is essential as without it, life is flat and dull. If you are laughing, then you are enjoying the present moment. Therefore, the more you laugh, the more you are living in the present. Increasing these moments will create a happier you.

Key Words:

Active * Enjoy * Laugh * Social * Feelings *Present

There are No Traffic Jams on the
Extra Mile

Code 3
See the Bigger Picture

Code 3: Find a purpose and a passion that enables you to focus on the bigger picture, while ignoring the daily negative distractions and people that can drown your ambition. Thrive in life with direction and purpose.

Scenario: Lisa has been studying media at college for two years and is enjoying her training. However, she strongly doubts whether she will be able to develop her passion into a full-time job; "Why should I be so lucky?" she questions. Lisa has been applying for media jobs for the last two months and has not received any positive responses. One day her dad's friend calls. "I've got a great opportunity for your daughter," he tells Lisa's dad, who relays the message to Lisa. The job is working for a Porsche dealership, selling cars to high-end customers. He explains the commission is 1 per cent for every car sold, plus there is a basic salary on top of this, and the use of a company car.

Now Lisa has always had a love of cars, and even with her basic numeracy skills she knows that 1 percent commission would equate to around £700 per sale, so her eyes light up. Two days later, the house phone rings again. This time, it's Lisa's lecturer from college. He has managed to get Lisa a work experience placement at a national newspaper; it is initially for three months, unpaid, but has the potential to lead to a full-time role. Lisa needs to make her decision by the end of the week.

Potential Outcome:

A) Take the car sales job and start earning a good income.

B) Take the work experience role and it leads to nothing other than good experience.

C) Take the work experience role and it leads to a full-time position.

D) Hesitate and both opportunities disappear.

Step Out from Mediocrity

"Having the big picture in mind enables us to overcome the day to day routines that attempt to distract us from pursuing our dream."
(*Assegid Habtewold*, The 9 Cardinal Building Blocks: For Continued Success in Leadership

The bigger picture can only be seen from zooming out. This means sometimes you will need to step back and evaluate your life to discover where it's going; only then can you decide what positive changes need to happen for progress to occur. In essence, if you can see the bigger picture you will live with a sense of what is important and what is not (most things).

I can give you an example: I am an uncle to two wonderful nieces and one amazing nephew. When I got my first-ever new (ish) car, an Audi A4, I drove it round to my sister's to collect the three children to take them to Chessington World of Adventures (a theme park in the UK). As I parked up, my sister walked out with a cup of tea, looked at me and said, **"Are you sure about taking them in that car? I wouldn't if I was you!"** I looked at her and then looked at the children's faces. They looked at me with a sense of disappointment; I could see the despair in their eyes. They loved cars and always wanted to ride along with me, I think mainly for my singing or maybe even my dancing. I smiled at my sister as I snatched the cup of tea out of her hand and threw its contents at the passenger's side door. It was a hot August day and the windows to my car were open just under halfway. The tea covered the outside of the passenger-side windows, the passenger seats and the gear stick. Everybody looked at me in shock and in stunned silence; they all walked up to the car to for a closer inspection. My sister broke the silence. **"Oh, I'd better make myself anther cup, then!"** With this, we all started to laugh.

My intention was to emphasise that the car meant nothing to me compared to my love for those children. Sure enough, all the children hopped in and displayed only joy about being in the car, devoid of any worry about spilling anything. The people in society who can't see that car as just the lump of metal it is will also refuse to see the bigger picture. Any possession, no matter how large or expensive, has no value in comparison to the memories and welfare of people; in this scenario, it was the memories of three children. We will all have memories of spilling something on a carpet or in a car as a child and getting duly disciplined for doing so. As time passes, we will still remember the feeling associated with the response we received as a result that action, even though the object we damaged is most likely irrelevant now to all concerned. I still have a strong memory stained in my mind. I was visiting my friend's family and his dad took us out in his brand new Mercedes-Benz. I had a chocolate milkshake in my hand (I think it was a Yazoo), and he made me promise not to open it. The temptation was too much. As I peeled off the lid from the top of the bottle, he sharply hit the brakes and the drink flew all over me, my friend and the backseat. I can still recall the telling off I received as it made me feel about two inches tall. However, that very car that I spilt my chocolate milkshake in is now lying dormant in a scrapyard somewhere. Do you see my point? When I threw a cup of tea into my brand-new car, I saw the bigger picture, which shocked those living in the smaller frame. That car won't be mine in ten years' time, but those children will remember that moment. Hopefully, they will repay me by making me cups of tea when I'm in an old people's home. Possessions are invented, designed and manufactured to assist our lives, to make our lives easier—not to control them or take the focus off of what is truly important.

In 2014 I slipped a disc in my lower back. It was debilitating and I was bedridden for four months. During this period, I did not desire a car, a new house, or a new phone ... no, all I wanted was to be pain-free and to be able to walk again. To me, being active again was priceless, and experiencing this vantage point has enabled me to put some life situations into perspective. At the time, I would have paid anything to be able to walk without pain and a limp. When your health or that of someone close to you is challenged, it strips away all other desires, allowing you to focus on what is important. A new pair of trainers that will be likely be destroyed within eight months are not as valuable as being able to walk without crying in pain. We are all already priceless; despite this fact, we are intent on constantly chasing better possessions or more money, while the true value remains within us. Imagine you had everything you desired in life by the time you were sixty years old. Along the way you had lost an arm. How much would you pay to have the arm replaced or repaired or even to be the age you are at this present moment?

If we take this philosophy to the extreme lengths, we are fundamentally asking ourselves if we would we rather be:

A. Poor and healthy?
B. Wealth and unhealthy?

The answer appears very obvious that health, both physical and mental, should be our priority in life. How many people do you know who continue to work through stress and anxiety in a job they dislike? Remember, if you are happy, then nothing else matters—especially such worthless tangible items like money and material possessions. The sooner we can understand and appreciate this strange and conflicting view of the world that we live in, the better our experience of life will become. Now I know having a comfortable life is important and it is something we all desire and aspire to possess. However, if this becomes the sole focal point of your existence, then I'm afraid you are missing out on life itself. You can accept this fact now or later in life, but the sooner you do, the more chance you will have of achieving a higher quality of life.

A key concept of focusing on the bigger picture is

the need to have a goal or a project you are working towards. I cannot place enough emphasis on the importance of finding a passion in life. (Hopefully you have unearthed one within your goal-setting task.) This purpose can literally be anything that appeals to you. It may be something you previously thought you were good at and able to achieve in, but unfortunately, society squashed that internal desire and self-confidence. I am telling you to ignore all negative voices (Negative Nigels) from both outside and from within. When you have a passion or a goal, work does not become your life; instead, work is a deterrent from what you really want to be doing. We must all make effective use of time off, both before and after work.

With a new focus, you will soon start forming positive habits and before you know it, you will be waking up before your alarm even sounds. Your day will become increasingly productive; you will have a buzz and independence that exudes from you. I once stopped my friend on a stag do; he was giving me stick about how much money he earned and what car he owned. I said, **"Andy, I have a job I love so I never have to work. I do not need to set an alarm as I am excited to get out of bed and before I have even**

got to work I have read a chapter of a book and completed a four-mile run. You can keep your money and your car .... I'm going to outlive you and look better for it!"

We both laughed. He has been one of my best mates since school, but everything I said to him that day was true. What's the difference between the man who crawls out of bed, has a cigarette, brushes his teeth and rushes into work, and the man who gets up early, exercises, reads and drinks a smoothie before going into work? Desire and focus. They both have the ability and opportunity to start the day positively, but only one of them has the desire to lead a productive self-evolving life. There is zero enjoyment in surviving through life; life is meant to be fun, innovative and spontaneous. Granted, it can't be like that all the time, but it can be more often than not. That all starts with setting a goal, finding a purpose and seeing the bigger picture. This change in focus from a zoomed-in narrow perspective to a zoomed-out larger perspective will allow you to see who needs to be in your life, what changes need to be made and what will allow you to map a clear path to your passion. The journey on the route to your dreams is a far more enjoyable one than the route to fulfilling other individuals' or corporations' plans and desires.

You are developing a purpose, and whatever this may be, however slow the progress you may experience is, you have a pathway to accomplishing it. You will hear negative voices from both the inside and outside, and people will question the changes they witness in you, but you must stay focused, stay in your zone. Staying focused is the best way to avoid unnecessary conflict. Being capable of seeing the bigger picture is also a useful tool in terms of resentment; it will dramatically reduce it. The more time you spend trying to get "one up" on someone else or seek revenge, the more you lose. It is the equivalent of carrying a full bucket of water around with you while attempting to knock over other people's buckets as they carry them home. Your aim is to reduce the volume of water that others have, but as you try to take from others, you will inevitably spill water from your own bucket, leading to frustration and more anger. Now ignore all the other people and focus on getting your bucket of water home. Once home, focus on returning, refilling and getting a second bucket home. The second bucket represents your personal growth, growth that was not achievable as you battled with resentment.

Revenge is a small-minded concept; forgiveness is for the advanced thinker, and this belongs to you and me. Revenge and anger will end up reflecting back onto ourselves. When I first started driving my 1998 Ford Fiesta around, I would get into road rage with other road users, threatening to pull over to argue with them, swearing at them and getting very angry. This emotion would stay with me all day, and nine times out of ten, this would ruin my day. I now drive a much better car (with a tea-stained front passenger seat) with far more power, but do I offer other drivers the opportunity to race or do I get angry when drivers cut in front of me? No. I am content that my car would beat theirs if I wanted to, and I am content in not allowing anybody to affect my mood. In fact, if I see them getting angry and abusive, I laugh. I laugh because they are wasting so much energy on a minor incident at seven in the morning, I think to myself, **"Wow, they're in for a long day."** These people can only focus on this very moment; they feel wronged and their ego takes over. Bigger-picture viewers let these moments wash over them, preventing it from impacting their day, other than creating feelings of sympathy for the red-faced angry driver and their unfortunate work colleagues.

Meaningless Media

Another way to see the bigger picture is to not only step back but step away from the crowd. How many hours do you spend worrying about irrelevant social media issues and problems? For me, social media has become like a smoking addiction for some. It takes the freedom away from your day as social media is constantly checked, stressed over and a focus of most discussions and gossip. When I deleted my Facebook account I felt an overwhelming sense of freedom. It also fulfilled my desire to be different, to quietly achieve without the scrutiny of others. It's important to have a self-worth, so much so that you do not need any outside reassurance. Step away from the masses that share the same video clips and photos, and the panic to be the first to wish somebody happy birthday or congratulate them on some achievement ... like I said, I gained a sense of freedom. I lead quite an interesting life, as I'm sure you do, and I'm pretty sure I know about it, as do my friends and family. My achievements will not increase in size if an extra two or two thousand people "like" them.

I recently had the opportunity to appear on a TV show here in the UK. The show will not be aired for around six months after the date of filming; therefore, I have been instructed not to mention the show. This whole experience gave me a strange feeling of power and pride. During this period, I witnessed social media updates about nights out, pictures of food and even what people had watched on TV. Hidden behind all this obscurity I quietly achieved something of note, something that only a few people close to me knew about. Of course, the other strange side of social networking is the connection of people on a virtual platform while in the domain of the real world a disconnect remains. Working in a P.E. office, we share lots of funny stories. Dale, who was a very funny teacher I once worked with, told me a story that still tickles me to this day: **"This bloke at my football club added me on Facebook the other day; he seems like a nice bloke, so I accepted."** "Fair enough," I thought to myself as I typed up a lesson plan at my desk. He continued. **"I saw him on Saturday night in the pub; he walked into the toilet as I was leaving. I asked him if he was all right and he just completely blanked me!"** I thought that this was a bit weird; after all, this guy had added Dale as a friend. I turned away from my laptop to face Dale and asked, **"Then what happened?"** now very interested. Dale continued. **"I left the toilet for about five seconds, then something switched in my mind and I marched back in there, pointed at him and shouted, THAT'S IT! YOU'RE BLOODY COMING OFF MY FACEBOOK!"** I literally rolled around on the floor laughing my head off. I think it was the pettiness of the situation, the awkwardness of someone adding you on a social network but not being able to speak to you in the real world, or maybe just the anger in Dale's voice.

I will repeat: all personal social media is irrelevant and should be treated as such. It is a game. It's the people we interactive with and come into contact with and that affect our lives for the positive that truly matter. Nobody is as their social profile depicts them; it is the best version of them. The profile pictures don't even match people's real-life image anymore ... so what's the long-term point in it all? Ultimately it's just a waste of time and energy. If I get my phone out when I meet up with one of my best friends, "Windy," he tends to quip sharply, **"No phones, just us!"** I always laugh and slowly tuck my phone back into my pocket. I have grown to enjoy this little saying. If I ever find myself sat with someone who finds their handset far more interesting than me, I now employ it. I recommend trying it; after all, it's no fun looking at the top of someone's head for any length of time, is it!?

There are many day-to-day distractions that keep us from living in the here and now. Thus, it is difficult to stay focused, but difficult is what we are looking for. It's easy to sit there on your phone and bury your head in a game or some app. It's time to start focusing on the company we are with, enjoying the moment, making the moment great—not just the online perception of the moment.

In this book, we are working on you becoming the best version of yourself. As this starts to occur, you will slowly lose interest in social media and become less reliant on it. There is an underlying irony to social media; who has the better life—the person who spends hours a day on Facebook, commenting, posting pictures and sharing stories, or the person who rarely logs on to it? Of course, the masses of non-code followers will not perceive it in this way. **"Alan hasn't been up to much lately,"** they will think to themselves as Alan quietly enjoys his life away from social updates. The same people who obsess over social media are the ones who invariably watch and post about talk shows, programmes that condemn the most uneducated members of our society. These shows are becoming increasingly popular as they serve to boost the self-esteem of the people who watch them; that is the main strength of shows that degrade the poorest members of our society. The non-risk takers of this world can sit back and judge others; it saves them having to work towards a goal as they can justify their existence in comparison to the victims that appear on these shows. When you attain a higher level of consciousness, self-approval and evaluation will be enough to keep you on the right track.

But what will I do if I delete my Facebook? How will people stay in touch with me!? The people who call or text you are your friends; try making a few phone calls to catch up with people. Imagine all the spare time you would have at your disposal. You could learn a language, how to play a musical instrument, or even get home and read ... yes, read! Reading will set you apart from most of your friends as you will develop knowledge and an interest in various topics, and your views and opinions will develop as you become more informed. Alongside this, stop watching TV. Yes, as crazy as it sounds, stop watching TV. Sport, films and documentaries are

OK, but for everything else, press that little red standby button. TV is the single biggest waste of your time and it inhibits personal development. The more TV you watch, the less you develop and grow and the more you slip into the realm of mediocrity and mindlessness.

Task 3: Reality Bites

I want you to go five days without watching TV and without using your phone for social media purposes. Alongside this, you are going to find another book to read on a topic of interest to you. Complete this task for just five days; then you can go back to normal if you wish. Five days out of a lifetime of TV and social media. I have included a table for you to record your progress:

Day	Comments	Enjoyment out of 10
1		
2		
3		
4		
5		

If you were unable to complete the challenge, let's think about why. I admit it is a difficult challenge, and one within this book I suspect most readers will struggle to complete. It's designed for you to start reflecting internally, helping you to become less reliant on external forces for your source of happiness. It is also a chance for you to find focus away from the white noise of society. Remember, time is precious, and social media and reality TV is a waste of this valuable commodity. This time away may have enabled you to start focusing on the three goals you established in Code 1.

Robots

"You have brains in your head. You have feet in your shoes. You can steer yourself in any direction you choose. You're on your own, and you know what you know. And you are the guy who'll decide where to go." (Dr Suess)

"Robots, robots everywhere," I thought to myself as I drove in to work early one morning. On the road is perhaps the clearest place to distinguish between those that follow life's secret codes, as described within these pages, and those that are mere cogs in life's giant wheel. It's 7:39 a.m. and I was waiting behind a small blue Nissan Micra for a good three to four minutes. Now, I was in no rush to get to work, even though I was desperate for my next caffeine hit. I was content to wait as this car in front of me, which appeared to be under the control of an elderly woman, was attempting to turn right into a narrow side road and across the flow of oncoming traffic. She was forced to wait patiently as cars whizzed past, not allowing her to turn. She started to creep out onto the other side of the road in a vain attempt to force the issue; she may have also been feeling pressured from the long line of cars building slowly behind her. I watched and watched in disbelief; gradually I started to smile, shortly followed by laughter at the irony of the situation. I was laughing in complete shock at the lack of manners and care for another road user—more importantly, a fellow human being. This little old lady just wanted to turn across traffic; it would have taken ten seconds for a car to stop and allow this to happen. As I looked in my rear-view mirror I could see the line of traffic at around twenty cars now growing and growing. All of us were waiting for a knight in shining armour to allow this elderly woman to turn. **"You shall not pass!"** screeched another car as it purposely sped up to reduce the gap between two cars, a gap that may have provided the slightest chance of letting the lady go on her merry way. I continued to laugh in disbelief at this singular, selfish mindset ... and then it dawned on me: these people are all just robots. They are afraid to make a decision that will go against the grain. Driving, like life, is easiest if you are just copying the actions of others. Making a decision to allow someone to pass would involve a thought process, that which only an individual would be prepared to make, knowing full well that the robot in the car behind would be greatly offended that you had allowed someone to pass. **"How dare you be courteous to another road user and delay my journey by three seconds ... I hate you!"** is the attitude that the car user behind you would display as they moved as close to your rear bumper as was possible. Here's where code followers, like yourself, differ: they do not care about the negative thoughts of strangers, as negativity will no more impact their day than a drop of rain splashing against the windscreen. They do the right thing by their own set of personal rules and principles; they are willing to break the mould in order to help out another person. This independent behaviour will only have a positive effect on one's self-image and self-efficacy. How many times have you been driving down a country road and the car behind gets too close behind you, so you speed up and they mimic your driving and speed up also!? I have gotten to a sharp corner before and dropped down the gears to whiz around in a tight turn without hitting the brakes and then watched in the rear-view mirror as the robot in the car behind, attempting to keep up, ends up on the wrong side of the road. It's like these people need constant guidance. Today, if a car gets too close behind me I now pull over and allow them to pass, forcing them to take charge of their own destiny. Robots also don't obey speed limits, because yet again that would involve some form of decision-making; they drive as fast as they can until something slows them down. Like in life, they have no real control over their journey; they are followers and have no codes to live by. Smile at these road users and let them pass, as they are in a hurry but, unfortunately, their journey has no direction, the sat nav has run out of batteries and they definitely don't know how to read a map.

Robots don't live and die by the sword; they don't trust their gut instinct or follow their dreams. They live a shell of a life dictated to by a greater power, they have little control over their day-to-day life and, hence, decision-making has become very rare. The weeks blend into one another as the normality of their life has no stand-out moments. They will have the odd holiday, which will be counted down to for months on social media networks and then after the event, you will be subjected to months of **"I wish I was back here"** statuses. Why do they look backwards? Because they haven't got the mindset to look forward to a new adventure; their next adventure will be next summer. It's a life on autopilot. I have nothing against these people; I just don't want you to be one them. If you are a robot or fear you are becoming one, then it's time to wake up! Start small by making decisions outside the norm or decisions that differ from the course of action you would be obliged to normally take. Some minor examples of this could be to get up a little earlier or take a different route to work, eat something different at lunchtime or go to the gym, stay at work until all your tasks are complete, challenge a friend to a game of squash or tennis after work, choose a random book to read in the evening and plan to write a small (but positive) review for it, call a distant family member for a chat ... something—anything—to break the confines of a robotic structure. Maybe some of these minor changes would be steps to a more humane existence. If you follow the same routine day in and day out, how can you expect things to improve or get better? The definition of madness is doing the same things over and over again and expecting the results or outcomes to be different.

> *"Good manners open the closed doors; bad manners close the open doors!"*
> — *Mehmet Murat ildan*

Robots struggle with other basic life concepts. Manners and walking are two pretty basic functions, you would imagine; however, to robots, these prove to be more of a challenge. I am many things, but I have been raised to be polite at all times to all people. I will always have a conversation with people who work in shops or behind counters. I am acutely aware that hiding behind that uniform is a real person with a family, friends and feelings ... yes, feelings! Next time you go into a shop, try asking the person serving you some questions: "How are you?" and "Have you had a good day?" This is something I have noticed that happens in every interaction in America; in the United Kingdom, we are less concerned with this verbal exchange of niceties. If you compare standing in a lift in the UK, where there is minimal eye contact and communication, to standing in an elevator in

America, you can see the difference between the two countries. In the USA, by the time the lift gets to the third floor, you will have made a new best friend. I'm not sure if this is a confidence thing, but communication definitely occurs more in America.

I enjoy these interactions with various members of staff, especially in restaurants. I do not like the feeling of someone waiting on me; I find myself constantly aware that this is a human being no better or worse than me. Robots, on the other hand, will treat these people with a certain sense of snobbery and discontent. They do not have the ability to engage in a conversation with anyone and, what's more, manners for the most hardened robots are a real challenge. It used to really antagonize me when I would let someone pass or smile at someone in the street and they would not be willing to acknowledge me as a human being; it's truly incredible. I think, for us non-robots, we need to develop habits to combat this. For me, I sing. Yes, that's right, I sing ... something my nan taught me.

Recent scenario: I'm leaving a building and I can sense a lady behind me. I turn to see she is carrying folders that are awkwardly resting on her crossed arms. As I approach the exit, I reach to grab the handle in order to hold the door wide open. **"After you,"** I state with a large smile on my face, and the lady looks at me and marches straight through the door! I quickly revert to my anti-robot combat tactic and I start to sing, **"Smile and the whole world smiles ... cry and you cry alone."** I sing loudly within earshot as I walk past the lady, who is unlocking her car door. A little personal victory against a robot for mankind everywhere and it may, just may, have helped plant a seed for the next time she is called upon to use some basic manners.

It's the same with the basic human function of walking. I can't count the number of times I have literally had to stop and stand still because the person heading towards me doesn't seem to have the cognitive function to control the direction of their feet. Sometimes I wonder if they have put their shoes on the wrong feet. You know the situation—it's obvious that they either have to slow down or wait a millisecond to allow the natural order of things to unfold, but they can't and we know why, don't we ... yep, basic decision-making, the major design fault with all robots. It's a similar process to driving, but these particular machines have a lot more water in their systems, as there must be a huge delay in the relay of messages within their switchboards. Some people believe that one day robots are going to take over the world; judging by the ones already roaming around society, I don't think we are in any danger of this happening ... do you!? Don't worry, I have another combat measure for these robots: I just smile, stop walking and force them to make a directional decision. I also use the word **"wow"** regularly in these occasions out of pure amazement. I do not get angry because we must never, I mean never, let a robot ruin our day, especially when the majority are out in force during commutes to and from work.

Robots also use public transport. I have witnessed many train, tube and bus users that refuse to give up their seats to elderly people or pregnant ladies. They just don't have the mental functioning to offer a helping hand to somebody who requires it. There are personal benefits to helping others that these people will not experience, not the least of which is by offering assistance it displays that you are not made of metal. If you witness somebody offer up a seat on public transport or helping to carry someone's buggy down the stairs, what feelings does this generate for you towards them? If I offer assistance to others, perhaps selfishly, it only serves to make me feel positive about myself. For you, and only you, are responsible for your own personal image in every single interaction throughout your day. Conversely, if I witness somebody else offer assistance to a passing stranger, I like to praise them: **"Well done,"** or **"That was a nice thing you did there, mate,"** just to acknowledge their positive contribution to the world. In summary, please don't be a robot. Make decisions that will benefit you and others around you.

Robin Hood Principle

> *"The way to happiness: Keep your heart free from hate, your mind from worry. Live simply, expect little, give much. Scatter sunshine, forget self, think of others. Try this for a week and you will be surprised."*
> — *Norman Vincent Peale*, The Power of Positive Thinking

Helping others is a wonderful thing, especially when we decide to aid those people that are less fortunate than ourselves. Many people in the world require some form of assistance, and not necessarily of monetary value. I myself am a blood donor, something I am very proud of. I started donating blood while my nan was in hospital for an extensive period of time. I witnessed firsthand how important blood is for hospital patients: my nan would receive a fresh supply of blood injected into her arm and this would cause her to perk up for a few hours. It became an essential part of her treatment. Unfortunately, my nan died during this spell in hospital and this loss took a piece of me with her; she was a hero to me. She was a true character and I think the first person I can remember that didn't care what anybody thought of her. I always respected her for that.

She once told me that when I was born, she was working in a large Farah clothes factory. As soon as she found out I was healthy and OK, she ran up to the tannoy system, barging past her boss, who spoke to the factory workers from a high tower, and she yelled, **"I'm going to be a grandma ... it's a boy!"** and all the workers applauded and cheered as she sheepishly walked back past her boss to the factory floor. I loved hearing this story. As I got older, I used to take her out for dinner in the evening and we would always have a laugh. After we had finished eating, we would get up to leave the restaurant and I would whisper to her, **"You're going to have to move a bit quicker than that, Nan ... I didn't pay."** We would both laugh and she would call me a little bugger!

I think now that we have a line of code followers in our family; my nan used to tell me that her dad would have loved me and my attitude towards life. During the war, the Germans were bombing around her estate in London and she would sit and nervously pray in the flat she lived. One day she turned to her dad and said, **"Are we going to be OK, Dad?"** to which her dad quickly replied, **"Don't worry, girl, if they bomb us they've gotta hit those miserable old buggers above us first!"** Laughter can be always be found, even in the darkest of places.

My blood donating began because of my nan, but continued for a number of selfish reasons. Firstly, it takes 650 calories to donate blood—yes, 650 calories, just like that! If you are dieting or looking to lose weight, get down your local blood bank. Secondly, it's quite a social thing as you can feel part of something good and everyone in there is helping a good cause. You will also receive free tea and biscuits, which is always nice; you will sometimes notice a few people lingering around this area of the donation station a bit longer than necessary. Thirdly, and most importantly, you will save a life. About two weeks after your donation, you should receive a thank-you letter stating that your blood has been donated to someone who desperately needed it. Fourthly, you will feel better about yourself. My self-esteem gets a huge boost once I have donated and I am proud to be able to do a good deed for others; this is referred to as the "Helper's High." The Helper's High is a similar feeling to that produced by visiting our two new best friends, laughter and exercise. That warm inner glow, knowing you have completed an act of kindness, like letting an old lady in blue Nissan Micra turn onto a side road, giving up your seat to a pregnant lady on a bus or opening a door for someone.

Donating money creates a similar response and will boost your self-image. How do you feel when you walk past a homeless person holding a sign? I always feel guilty. I know I shouldn't always feel this way, but secretly I do. I don't always donate directly to homeless people as I know the importance of donating to a trustworthy charity. Any functioning empathetic human being will feel a sense of injustice as they march off to Costa Coffee or Starbucks to buy a £3 latte while there are people begging on the street;

it's a horrible image. This happens every day, day in and day out, and it is very sad. I have often thought I would like to sit with a homeless person for a while, talk to them and experience a day in their shoes. I haven't summoned up the courage yet, but I think it would be a worthwhile exercise to increase my understanding of their situation; they are human beings, even though most of us, myself included, refuse to offer any assistance. So, if we can deduce there is guilt attached to not donating, then there must be some intrinsic reward for donating ... makes sense, right?

If you walk past a homeless person on your way to work, I challenge you to spend one week ignoring them, as you may well normally do, followed by a second week of donating 50p/50c every day, Monday to Friday. Subsequently, I would like you to assess in which week you feel better about yourself. Imagine both scenarios now—walking hurriedly past a man on the footpath in Week 1 without making eye contact, experiencing feelings of guilt and sadness. Conversely, in the second week, you donate 50p to the man, who will hopefully thank you, and other people on your commute will witness this donation, inducing a feeling or pride. Other people have all walked past, yet you have donated; therefore, you are more caring than them. Maybe that's taking it a bit far, but I can sense the positive responses from donating, not least the increased view of your own self-worth. Ironically, by giving to others or a charity, we are topping up our own self-esteem pool; in essence, we give to get more back. Helping others releases feel-good energy within us while boosting our own self-image. It is ingrained in human nature to help others in need, and fighting against this has a detrimental effect on our own self-worth. Try donating on your commute for a week and judge this for yourself. Start to dismantle that robotic outlook on life.

Moaners & Groaners

"Any fool can criticize, condemn and complain—and most fools do."
— *Dale Carnegie,* How to Win Friends & Influence People

The epitome of not seeing the bigger picture, by deduction, is only concentrating on the smaller picture. What is the smaller picture? This means your focus is constantly on the next task at hand. Many people don't plan on longer-term career goals and certainly don't have a passion that drives them forward. They have stopped learning and growing and truly believe they are the finished article; they feel that they know enough to get by, and they probably do. If you just want to get by and you are happy with the progress you have made in your life, then by all means stop reading now. This book is not aimed at you.

Have you ever had a bad day as an individual or as part of a group or team? Who are the weakest people in the room? The moaners. The easiest thing in any environment is to moan. It takes no effort to moan and complain, and literally everybody is capable of it. If you have ever had a bad experience on holiday or at a restaurant, you would be far more likely to write a negative report than you would be to write a glowing reference if you had been provided with an amazing time.

Moaners and groaners surround our lives like bad smells; they attempt to impact our thought process like bacteria entering our bloodstream. When bacteria infect our system's white blood cells and antibodies fight to eradicate it, the same process should occur for negativity; our mind should fight and destroy these thoughts. Most moaners and groaners do so behind people's backs as they are predominantly cowards; if they were ever challenged about their stance, they would shy away like they ultimately do for most challenges in life. If you have a friend who moans about others to you, make no mistake, they are also moaning about you to other people.

Groaners are negative people; they struggle to develop any real bonds with others as they cannot switch off the negative viewfinder. These complainers are far too afraid to try anything new and, therefore, struggle to find a passion in life; they are reactive rather than proactive individuals. After all, it is far easier to knock others and speak ill of them from afar than attempt and possibly fail at a challenge themselves. You must remember that some people hate seeing others progress; they will try to infiltrate your progress, for they cannot see the bigger picture that you can see and they will not definitely not understand your vision. They live in such a small frame that the thought of a larger goal scares them or appears so far away from their starting point that they give up readily. Seeing the bigger picture helps you to set large goals and be proactive; these goals may have once seemed too distant, but because of your new vantage point, they are now always in your frame. Moaning and complaining are not the qualities of leaders and independent thinkers.

Challenge

The Mona Lisa

Can you go one day without moaning, groaning or complaining? I want you to select a day, preferably a working day. During this day, on your phone or in your notebook, attempt to keep a record of the number of times you moan or complain. You can also make a record of the time this occurred and, if you wish, what the moan was regarding.

Complain Ta~~lly~~: | | | | | | **Total:** 7
Time & Reason:
1) 7:07 a.m. Because...
2) 7:39 a.m. When.....

At the end of the day, tally up your score. It may shock you how often you complain, but what I hope is more shocking is the way that this makes you feel. We have examined the impact a negative dialogue with other people has upon our mindset; there is a correlation between these emotions and self-moaning.

If your internal dialogue is negative, then your ducklings (emotions) will also be. We have started to adapt our external dialogue by being "fantastic" and sending out positive emotions; if we can achieve this same process internally, using positive attachments, then we are creating a strong positive bubble or shield. As the process of positive attachment becomes habitual, you will be able to stop wearing an elastic band on your wrist or picturing bananas; you will also witness a decline in moaning and groaning.

Knight Knight

Two knights are standing on a large hill overlooking a vast forest; they cling tightly to their horses. They have been travelling for three days and are extremely low on water supplies. It is an overcast day and visibility of the forest below is poor. The two knights discuss their plan of action. The silver knight states that he plans to stay on the hill and rest his loyal steed while he waits for visibility to improve so that he can plan a direct route to the nearest lake or stream. The black knight agrees.

"OK. I think we should get moving, but I will follow your suggestion." They wait and wait. Three hours pass by and the black knight is becoming increasingly restless. "We are wasting time; I am thirsty." The silver knight replies, "I too am thirsty. Focus on the fresh air and enjoy the rest; we will be on our way again shortly." The black knight grunts in agreement. Another two hours pass and some clinking of armour awakens the silver knight from his rest. "Where are you going?" he asks the black knight as he straddles his horse. "I'm going for water. This is useless; we are wasting time," replies the black knight as he rides off down the east side of the hill. The silver knight stops and contemplates his situation. He decides to wait and continues to rest. Two hours later he awakens to a clear blue sky; he can see as far as the eye can see. He notices two lakes. One has fresh water streaming from a glorious waterfall and, in fact, the whole area is a bright, vibrant green colour. The other is in a gloomy part of the forest; the trees appear barren and the area is sparse. The silver knight heads down the west side of the hill to the fresh water source, eager to hydrate himself and his faithful horse. They both continue on their journey fully rested, hydrated and alone. The black knight was never seen again.

If you act without fully understanding all the possible outcomes at some stage, this will cause an abrupt end to your journey. The bigger picture may not always be instantly apparent, but if you wait and carefully assess the situation, it will become clear. The silver knight understood the importance of rest for both the body and the mind while planning a clear pathway to his goal. Moaners and groaners cannot show patience; they have their opinion and are unable to reflect. They act hastily without collecting all the necessary information.

Lesson: When you have an idea of the bigger picture, smaller distractions cannot knock you off-course. You become acutely aware of what's important on your quest to a greater goal. You start to understand the actions of others, but realise that they are living day-to-day while you are planning for a greater outcome. This sense of purpose provides you with a resilience that will go undeterred as you follow your chosen path. Most people only possess one piece of the jigsaw puzzle; you will hold the completed version in your mind's eye.

Key Words:

Plan * Passion * Purpose * Positive

* Belief *Independent *Leader

Quick Test:

Q. How Are You?

Answer:

A. Fantastic

B. Fantastic

Or

C. Fantastic

Code 4
Family & Friends First

Code 4: Family should always be your main priority, get to know them, understand their views and always show them respect. The quality of the friendships and the bonds that you create along your journey through life will depict everything about you and your character. Trust people, show kindness where you can and forgive often.

Scenario: Chris always forgets to return phone calls from his mum. "She is probably moaning about something," he thinks to himself. He is an independent man who has a busy job; family life has become a distraction to him and his progress. One day he checks his phone; it displays "3 missed calls," all from home. "I'll call back later on," he decides. That evening, his mum calls again. This time, he answers and his mum says in a soft voice, "I needed you today. Your granddad has died."

Potential Outcome:

A) Chris feels guilty and decides to start putting more emphasis on friends and family.

B) Chris feels he couldn't have affected the outcome of the day and he does not change his ways or his focus in life.

Learn to Prioritise

Nothing is as valuable as spending time with friends and family—nothing! I'm sure you will have seen the very common film plot of a hard-working dad trying to make money for his family. The mum is at home growing increasingly unhappy and the kids never get to spend time with their dad. The dad, though his intentions are good, is working long hours to attempt to bring wealth and happiness into their home; he suffers from stress and anxiety most days. In many films, this scenario escalates to the wife's impromptu visit to the husband at work where she bursts into his office at the precise moment a young, attractive secretary kisses him on the lips. He does not kiss her back, yet it's too late for excuses and the wife storms out. I'm sure you can picture the scene. So what's the solution? The husband needs to be home more—obvious, right? "Yes, but he needs the money," you might be thinking ... but what for!? What is the purpose of making money if it is not creating happiness? Here lies the major problem with the real world today; only a few people will fully understand this concept.

Happiness is what we desire most, yet we spend our lives chasing something that ultimately causes more stress and unhappiness for ourselves and those around us. Happiness and contentment are not guaranteed when we reach a certain level of income. Money is not, and has never been, a requirement of being happy. However, we are all programmed to believe in the power of wealth from a young age, from the clothes we wear to the car our parents drive or the neighbourhood we live in. As crazy and as farfetched as it may seem, some of the happiest people on the planet are the poorest. In the film scenario described, the eager drive for money is not making anyone happy; it is the husband's ego and vision of happiness that is creating unhappiness and, ultimately, divorce. Money is overrated and time is greatly underrated. Spend time with your friends and family; make space for these people in your life as they are integral parts of life's puzzle. As you age, I guarantee you will gladly swap any pile of money accumulated in exchange for just a few more minutes or hours with loved ones or some of the people you have shared memories with. Take advantage of the present. Possessions have a price tag and are all replaceable, whereas people and memories are irreplaceable and priceless.

"Home is where you are loved the most and act the worst."
— *Marjorie Pay Hinckley*

If you are lucky enough to have close friends and family members in your life, then start today. Visit them, call them and most of all, respect them. Home is where the facade fades away, but that shouldn't mean you take out a day's frustration on your loved ones. I've never understood how someone can smile politely at the guy in the petrol station or in a supermarket, have a discussion about their lives and be friendly only to get back into the car or return home and be rude to their husband, wife or kids. We live in a bizarre world where people are too afraid to be impolite to complete strangers, but will happily get home and tell their partners to take a hike or, worse, ignore them.

It's very easy to lose perspective with family and even friends; we take them for granted and refuse to make as much time for them as we should. Families are forever and we must remember that; maybe that's why we push them as far as we can, because we know deep down there is an unbreakable bond. As discussed, some jobs force people to be polite and courteous all day, so when they get home, they erupt or ignore people. It's a bit like being a comedian— being funny all day and making hundreds if not thousands of people laugh, only to come home to be miserable, allowing that mask to rest for a few hours before turning the humour back on. We live up to the expectations of others in the real world, and once home, the mask slips and we show our true colours to friends, but more so, our family. How many of you burp, break wind or pick your nose at work!? I bet when you get home, there's not a moment of doubt when you need to complete one these basic functions from the comfort of your own couch.

We all wear a mask, but some people's masks are coated far more heavily than others. The thicker the mask you wear, the more the real you gets buried. Masking your personality eventually leads to stress and frustration that is, sadly, propelled at our nearest and dearest. Think about this next time you get into a shouting match with your mum, dad, sister or brother; ask yourself, "Is it them, or am I just venting anger from my day at work or college towards them?"

The Greatest Honour

I hope one day that any reader who has purchased this book is provided with the opportunity to be involved in a friend's wedding. More so, I hope you get to play one of the respective big roles. No, I'm not talking about the bride or groom—anybody can achieve this status. I'm referring to the two most exclusive roles of the day: the best man or chief bridesmaid. I have been lucky enough to have been best man six times in my life (but who's counting). I have also had the honour of representing the father of the bride for my younger sister. If I were to be asked what my greatest achievement in life is, then I would say it is these moments. If you are an older brother, I'm sure you can imagine the pride in walking your younger sister down the aisle; after all, you have probably spent years fighting her battles so it's nice to get a little something back ... plus, the free bar didn't go amiss. I'm sure you can also imagine how it feels to be asked to be the best man or chief bridesmaid, and the feelings of responsibility, pride and honour that are deeply connected with this request.

I can remember every best man speech I have made, every wedding venue where these occurred and I can also remember every time I have been asked to fulfil the role. My reaction to being asked has always differed. The first time I got asked by my childhood friend John, he turned to me and said, **"Are you crying!?"** and I was a bit, plus I had some dust in my eye or something. I knew it was a privilege not afforded to everybody, and I could feel the sense of honour attached to this question. As a best man, there are only a few minor tasks to complete: you need to make everybody laugh but not push these boundaries too far, make sure the groom doesn't pass out at the altar, look after the wedding rings and basically not ruin the biggest day of your friend's life! It sounds daunting and, at first glance, it is, but I have loved every one of them and I can honestly say they have all gone really well. I think I might create a book on this topic one day, to help others who have been asked to undertake the role to complete it with confidence.

Of course, alongside some of the duties mentioned on the day of the wedding, there's also the small matter of the stag do (or bachelor party). I have organised vineyard tours in Valencia, shooting ranges in Krakow, comedy clubs in Bournemouth and five-day trips to Vegas (which pretty much covers everything). I have loved every stag do I have both organised and attended. One surprising factor with all of them is the fact that there are the opportunities available to create bonds with people from different generations. I love to learn from other people, and stag dos provide this as fathers and fathers-in-law are often included in the celebrations. I respect older people, as I know this will soon be me; I enjoy their company and try to learn as much as possible from them. They are usually in a financially comfortable position, and if you listen carefully, they drop pearls of wisdom in most (sober) conversations.

"If you hang out with chickens, you're going to cluck and if you hang out with eagles, you're going to fly."
(Steve Maraboli, Unapologetically You: Reflections on Life and the Human Experience)

To be selected as best man or chief bridesmaid is a great honour and privilege. It means you have affected somebody's life in a positive way. You are engrained in their memories and you will now forever be intertwined in their life. The best thing about this process is that you have been given a job simply by being yourself. The clothes you wear, the phone you have, the car you drive—none of that matters; friends like you for you and all that you stand for.

What personality traits would you look for in a best friend? I think most of us would like friends who show characteristics such as kindness, honesty, a sense of humour and generosity; predominately, friendship should be based on who we are and how we act alone. Friendships based on pretence or social status are not genuine or beneficial to our lives, and fake bonds ultimately do not possess a solid base to lean on. Putting this into perspective, the greatest honour you can have in life is ascertainable to anyone from any social standing, as it is judged solely upon one's character. It is important to have a person, outside of your family, who holds you in high regard, but we spend so much time and focus on attempting to impress irrelevant people. When we look back on our lives, the judgement on our worth will be made by our close friends and family and how they have remembered us, so we must ensure we always do right by them. As the years pass us by, we will not reflect on our lives and think, **"I wonder what John in Accounts or Jane in the post office thought of me? Hope they liked me."** Put bluntly, if you died tomorrow, who would be at your funeral? Who would be there just to show face and who would be there devastated? Who would be the ones returning year after year to lay flowers? It's just a thought I sometimes have. Granted, it's a bit morbid, but it helps keep me grounded and prioritise my time and people. We only gain intrinsic rewards in life from being true and genuine to ourselves, whether this is putting effort into a business or a friendship. I warn you, do not live a life surrounded by fake friends or one that is untrue to yourself; this is a complete waste of time and will result in loneliness. Many people out there, unfortunately, do not see the bigger picture as you are beginning to. These people do not possess any real substance to their characters and there is a lack of humility and dignity. Drop them quickly and move forward; deep in your heart you know that they are not going to be there for you when the going gets tough.

Fake friends talk about you behind your back,

don't reply to messages and go to functions or events without inviting you. These people are the poison of many childhoods, yet I don't blame them as they are merely caught up in the smaller picture, only focusing on a fraction of what is happening day to day. These are the very people who use these vague Facebook status updates at least once a month: **Status:** "Best News Ever!!" or "Why always me!?" **Typical Response:** "What's up, hun!?" or 'What is it....excited!! (Smiley face)" **Reply:** "Oh nothing, just one of those days, call you later," or "So exciting, I'll text you now x". Dislike! Attention-seeking without substance: **'is this how you get your dopamine hit!?'** should be the only comment that is typed under this form of facebook status. If you had some good news such as you had won a holiday or had just got accepted into university, you would state this, right!? Social media is irrelevant, used most by those living frame-to-frame. You are starting to see the bigger picture, and this includes friendship groups. Go out and get as many real friends as you can from different social groups. In my experience, you can never have too many genuine friends in this world.

I have learnt a great deal from my friends as they all have a variety of skills and opinions. I love the huge range of my friendship group and the variety of interests encompassed within them; some like to play golf, some want to go to Vegas once a year, some enjoy the cinema and some love clubbing. A large friendship group gives you options. These people are the ones you turn to outside of your family for advice and help. True friends back you to the hills, and will be there for you at a drop of a hat.

University was a breeding ground of friendships for me; some of my best friends have come from my time there. I believe that, as you go through the educational system, the catchment of your friendship group slowly narrows, until it peaks on your course at university where most of the people enrolled will have some similar interests to you. At school, you are just dumped into the nearest one to your home, at college you choose your course and the type of college you want to go to, and by university you have chosen a more specific course and university. By my logic, there will be people on the course who have taken a very similar route as you did and, therefore, you have a foundation of shared interests. The working world should further narrow the group of people that fit in with your growth mindset—that is, of course, only if you get to do the job you want you to want in life. Otherwise, it's back to square one, and a random mix of people who haven't found an interest or purpose in life ... yet, I might add. A positive mindset will help you gain this purpose, and positivity is far more forthcoming if you have a strong friendship and family base.

Task 4: Positive People

List three positive people you have met in your life. These can be friends, family members, teachers, tutors, sports coaches or, indeed, anybody that has created a positive impact on your life.

3 Positive People	Reason for Choice
1.	
2.	
3.	

You will hopefully have two or three people that have had or continue to have a positive impact on your life ... keep these people in mind during your journey, talk to them and make contact with them regularly if you can. I have informed friends and family in the past that I refer to them when I require a positive lift in my life; this knowledge gives them a huge self-esteem boost and also tightens the bond between us. You will never regret spreading positivity; after all, what goes around comes back around.

Family Fun Days

As we grow and develop, we all go through various relationship stages with our families and, predominantly, with our parents or carers. As a young child, we are completely dependent on the care of others. In return, we offer unconditional love, as it is offered to us. As we grow and develop, we discover the joys of playing and laughter. We find intrigue and interest in the most mundane of tasks; at a young age, even the smallest of stimuli would get our creative juices flowing. Life was fun, with no responsibilities and without any judgement being made upon us.

I remember taking my nephew Jack swimming one holiday; he had made a friend named Ewan and they both loved swimming. As we finished getting ready we walked out into the main changing room area where Ewan was stood. **"Are you ready, Jack?"** he said with a huge grin on his face. It was at this point I noticed Ewan only had two fingers on his right hand, as did Jack: **"What happened to your hand?"** he asked Ewan in an innocent tone. Ewan replied, **"Oh, I had an accident when I was younger."** Jack responded, **"Does it hurt?"** Ewan replied, **"It did, but it's fine now."** Jack then said, **"OK, you wanna go swim?"** and they both ran and jumped into the pool, which was quickly followed by a sharp whistle from the young lifeguard dressed all in red.

I love the innocence of youth and the lack of judgement and preconceptions that are attached to being a child. Children enjoy each moment and live only in the present. Try to spend some time with some young people. If you have some in your family, great; if not, maybe volunteer to work at a local charity or sports club. Simply being around a positive and carefree attitude will definitely generate an impact on your mental health and wellbeing.

As we enter our teenage years, family sadly

becomes less of a priority and, if we are honest with ourselves—remember, we are reflective thinkers now—we would admit that during this stage of our development, we neglect them the most. This is the stage where arguments are a daily occurrence as life both inside and outside the home is stressful. We are evolving quickly during this phase both physically and mentally; external and internal stressors are forcing us to adapt. We are trying to find out who we are and where we fit into society. Looks and personal appearance are heavily relied upon by society, and it is within these years that we discover if we are good-looking or not. We are judged in all areas of our life and it becomes a negative phase for a while. I label this the "caterpillar stage" of our development, as we may have spots, braces and hairs that slowly appear in various locations and we are forced to grin (or snarl) and bear it for a few years. Our focus is on surviving and not thriving as we search for who we are; all family issues become a distraction as friendship groups become our main focus. Social networks and media are extremely important and heavily relied upon as we crave reassurance from outside our family setting. This is just a phase for all code followers; however, for some, this development stage is more than that. Part of their progression halts and they take many of these characteristics with them throughout their entire lives. As we exit this testing phase, we hit sixteen to eighteen years old, and the real world comes charging at us...

Through your twenties and thirties, true friends you have made along the way stay with you and your family will be the safe harbour you return to when your ship is leaking or requires repair. You are now working or studying, gaining an increased independence and, at this stage, the family unit is one of sanctuary. It is a safe base for you to return to when you need a place to be loved and cared for unconditionally. I learnt the most about my family during this stage, regarding moving out of the home, decorating, being responsible with money and setting goals. I became friends again with my parents. This sounds strange, but I think you eventually start to see them as real people and not just verbal punching bags. After moving away from home, I started to understand their backstories and their perspectives; moreover, I had developed more empathy towards them. It's a special phase and one you must enjoy. Try to visit them often or, at least, call them once every few days.

I have discovered that spending time with parents or grandparents is all they really desire; this is win-win as we should by now love their company. Instead of presents that would not be used, my mum has a drawer full of earrings and necklaces I have bought for her over the years. I now take family members to events, such as the theatre or for meals out. It is a much better use of money and gives us both memories to share; remember, they are aging too and before you know it, taking them into a city for a day may not be feasible. Take advantage of now ... in fact, I advise you to stop reading and call a family member now; tell them the book you are currently reading told you to. Especially make this call if there is someone you have argued with or have an ongoing grudge with; this may be the best thing you do this week or month. Revenge and resentment are self-deprecating, so remember, the longer this lasts, the more water you are spilling from your bucket.

Finally, we will enter the latter stages of life as we retire and find other hobbies to occupy our time, such as bowls. I often think about life as an old man and what this will involve; I just pray I have enough memories to last me during these latter years. I often feel sorry for Uncle Albert in *Only Fools and Horses* with his "During the war..." speeches that got ridiculed in TV programme by Del Boy and Rodney. If you are unsure who Uncle Albert is, then try to relate his character to one of your own family members. He always had a story, mainly war-related, to tell about something he had done or achieved in the past, and nobody in his family would take any notice in what he was saying. We are a fortunate generation; as we age, no one will ever doubt our generation's stories or what has been achieved in our lifetimes. One word: Instagram. Granddad/Grandma, did you really fight a lion? **"Check my Instagram."** Auntie, did you really scale Everest? **"Check my Instagram."** Uncle. did you really date a supermodel? **"Check my Instagram**." Seriously, how funny are social networks going to be as we get older? It's a complete history of our lives, available at the touch of a button. Scrapbooks and Polaroid pictures will be redundant, as all the evidence will be on social media in full colour.

Lesson: Friends and family are the most important things in our lives. The sooner we realise the value of family members and friendships, the greater the emphasis that we will start to place on them. Their worth overshadows any and all possessions and money accumulated. The impact that we have on the lives of others is the only way we will be remembered. Memories will one day be all we have, so start making or adding to them now and, what's more, focus on making them great.

Key Words:

Love * Trust * Character * Support *Genuine

What I'm after can't be purchased
online...

Code 5
Tales of a Time Traveller

Code 5: Fast-forward in time to analyse the outcomes of your decisions and life. Will the future you be proud of the pathway you're currently taking? What will you remember and be remembered for? Time is the most valuable currency we possess; do not waste it on anything other than the pursuit of your heart's desires.

Scenario: While looking back on his life, Fred, now sixty years old but still in good health, deeply regrets not taking the time to go to Niagara Falls, a childhood dream of his.

Potential Outcome:

A) He will live and die with this regret.

B) He sets some time to go and complete his childhood ambition.

Live Life Backwards

"I want to live my life in such a way that when I get out of bed in the morning, the devil says, "aw sh*t, he's up!" (Steve Maraboli, Unapologetically You: Reflections on Life and the Human Experience)

When I was fourteen I was sat in a Religious Education class at secondary school. The teacher was asking all the students what they desired from life. **"A Ferrari,"** said one of my classmates. **"A big house with a swimming pool**," said another. **"A fit bird**," said a third. As the teacher continued to ask this question to non-forthcoming students around the room, she paused her scanning of the class at my good friend Ben. Ben always had a different view of the world to others; he was argumentative at times but was also a very intelligent lad who rarely got flustered. **"I want to be happy,"** he said. The teacher replied, **"Yes, that's obvious, but anything else!?"** Ben quickly responded, **"What do you mean? I don't think that's a valid question."** The teacher, now with a stern expression, said: **"Well, what does happiness look like to you? Do you have a nice car? Nice house? Pretty wife?"** Ben smiled. **"I don't know, but if I'm** happy, then nothing else matters. I don't know what this will look like, but I will feel it when I get there." This memory has always stayed with me. I can remember the classroom, the teacher and the exchange of words between herself and Ben. Maybe even at the time an important memory is being created, our mind is aware of this fact. Maybe this ensures that it is stored into our long-term memory, or maybe it is just the shock of something different occurring that determines whether or not it is forgotten.

Ben was looking ahead, or looking back, depending how you perceive it—perhaps not to his death, but to himself as an older man. Thinking in this manner can help us get the most out of life. What will the older version of me be proud of? This is a question I ask myself at least once a week. One day I will be old, less mobile and less focused on my life, so I want to do all I can while I can. Sometimes we have to become time travellers within our own lives. I'm not talking about going back and changing the past; this time machine only goes one way ... and where we're going, we don't need roads! The future is the only place for us to suitably judge our lives and the current path we find ourselves on.

Take a few minutes now to fast-forward to an older image of yourself. Imagine sporting a checked cardigan with some dark grey slippers on and a bag of Werther's Originals in your pocket. (Maybe I've gone into too much detail, but you get the idea.) Take a look back on your life as it stands right now. What do you see? What have you achieved? What accomplishments would you be proud of? I often stop and do this, especially if a crossroads presents itself in my life. It's smart to attempt to consider all the outcomes almost as an outsider, from a neutral vantage point. Now, I'm not suggesting that every time there is a decision to be made, you grab Doc Brown and hop into the DeLorean, fire up the Flux Capacitor and whizz off. However, if you have a big call to make it can be a very useful tool. I like to combine this process with a quiet spot, outside in the fresh air. In fact, I recommend taking a bit of "you time" every so often, again ideally outside in a large open space; it's a nice way to collect all your thoughts without the distractions of modern society. I think some of my biggest decisions in life have been made on a park bench with a nice view. Not all of them correctly, I might add, but I can't blame the rural setting for my own misgivings.

The time machine, if used wisely, can help you to dramatically reduce the opportunity for regrets to sneak into your mind during the latter stages of your life. Imagine being in a wheelchair or having to use a walking stick and thinking, **"I wish I had done that bungee jump in Brazil,"** or **"Why didn't I take that snowboarding holiday to Norway?".** Add to this the feeling of knowing with absolute certainty that you will never get the chance to experience these countries and activities. I implore you, do not let this happen. If an opportunity arises and it feels right, then go for it. Challenge yourself, especially when it comes to travel. Travel is one of best self-development tools we have; you can learn vast amounts about other cultures, traditions and yourself. Travel will teach you how to be independent and responsible for yourself, as well as how to keep safe and increase your self-awareness. If you get the opportunity to go somewhere new, then go for it. Make that older version of you proud. Travelling will provide you with fond memories as you age, and these will be with you forever. Live a life so full of these memories and experiences that when you get older, you can look back and enjoy them all for a second time.

I phoned my mum up recently and told her of my desire to complete Route 66 in America one day. She replied, **"I've always wanted to do Route 66, but I know now I will never get the chance to. Your granddad needs looking after, and Dad's ill. I will never get the chance now."** This made me sad and I told her so. She replied, **"Well, the lesson here is to take your opportunities, son; they may not come round twice. Like all really good opportunities, there is a limited time frame to act."** We can only imagine what our thoughts and feelings will be as we age, but if you can do this with an open mind, it will definitely impact the way you live in the present. Hopefully, just like buying a raffle ticket, it will allow you to take a certain amount of measured risk.

"In my next life I want to live my life backwards. You start out dead and get that out of the way. Then you wake up in an old people's home feeling better every day. You get kicked out for being too healthy, go collect your pension, and then when you start work, you get a gold watch and a party on your first day. You work for 40 years until you're young enough to enjoy your retirement. You party, drink alcohol, and are generally promiscuous, then you are ready for high school. You then go to primary school, you become a kid, you play. You have no responsibilities, you become a baby until you are born. And then you spend your last 9 months floating in luxurious spa-like conditions with central heating and room service on tap, larger quarters every day and then Voila! You finish off as an orgasm!" (Woody Allen)

Living life backwards is an interesting concept in theory; it seemed to work out OK for Benjamin Button. However, what if we accidently time travelled too far into the future and we witnessed our own funerals? (Be careful with the control panel!) As crazy as this sounds, it might not be a bad thing ... well, not a totally bad thing. Once you accept that death is inevitable, it eradicates all fear.

Think back to a memory or a moment in time that made you feel really embarrassed and that perhaps left you vulnerable (like your trousers falling down in front of the whole school). Maybe even at the time of this embarrassment, you said to yourself, **"I just want to do die."** Looking back now, imagine if you had! Imagine if a large bolt of lightning appeared flying out the sky and struck you down. As you reach the gates of heaven (positive thinking) and God is standing before you, he says, **"Well, you got your wish!"** What would your reply be? Probably something like, "What a stupid way to go," or "It wasn't worth dying over," or "I've wasted my life." These are the overriding emotions that should take control when you feel insecure, embarrassed or unconfident—it's only a stupid thing / it's not worth stressing over / I'm missing an opportunity because of this. These moments of vulnerability happen to everyone all over the world, but those who fully accept that everyone's life will come to a conclusion interpret these circumstances differently. Accepting that the final curtain call will happen for you at some point puts everything into perspective. You start to realize that almost all of what you worry and stress over is irrelevant. In the grand scheme of things, we are all here for a very short time, a blip in history. At this moment, the world is ours to navigate and explore, but it doesn't ever really belong to us as a generation; we are all just passing through. As we age, a new generation starts their journey through the cycle of life and the process continues.

Now, being morbid is not my intention (even though I did mention funerals and dying—sorry) but if you think about this for a second—and really think about it—it should provide you with a sense of freedom. We are only going to be here for a short period of time, so why not live without fear and make an impact on this world? Leave your mark. You only get one shot, so either live with passion or drift by with fear. Try to lose the trait of being embarrassed; remember, those people that are judging you do so because you are doing or have done something unique, and it's the unique people whose memories live on.

Task 5: No Regrets

List two things that you know you would regret, if you failed to experience or attempt them during your lifetime. Fast-forward to the latter chapters of your life and reflect on past achievements—what would you want to be included amongst those memories? What have you always wanted to do or where have you always wanted to go?

Event	Why did you want to do this?	What is stopping you now?
1		
2		

Erase Embarrassment

"**Stop it, Peter! When are you going to grow up!?**" my mum would state firmly to me on regular occasions. Following this negative comment aimed towards me, I would smile and laugh. This phrase would be made after I had done something silly like singing to a cashier in a shop, attempting a magic trick to random people as we shopped or pretending to "do a runner" at a restaurant and not pay for the meal.

These are all just small and extremely immature acts, but I have always been able to do silly stuff like that without feeling an ounce of embarrassment. This feeling has been and gone throughout my life. In my teens, there was a sense of embarrassment for a couple of years; I can remember hating this feeling. The embarrassment flaw came back to me once again during my first year at university. I can remember waking up at university on occasions throughout my first six months there and being scared to walk around the campus. I was embarrassed at what had happened the night before, the silly antics from the night before and who would be laughing at me. I would bump into people who would say, "Oh my God, you were dancing on the tables last night," or

"You poured a pint on your head last night," and I used to think, "**Oh no, how embarrassing.**" I would also be concerned with my clothes—how I dressed and looked. Then one day, I woke up and something just clicked. I just don't care! I don't care what anybody thinks about me as they are all just like me, going out, being silly and making mistakes, or perhaps they are too afraid to. I would rather be the one dancing with a tie around my head than part of a loud mass of normality, gossiping about people like me who step out from the mould. It's good to lose your inhibitions and forget the fear of judgement from others. On your deathbed, you will want to know that you played the game of life to its fullest and didn't merely watch from the sidelines. I will have lived my life like I knew this day was coming and I will lie there with no regrets. I am not advocating getting drunk and wearing outrageous clothes while not caring about the consequences. Instead, I encourage you to learn how to deal with embarrassment. Learning about how to deal with embarrassment helped me to take this philosophy into my life post-university, allowing me to step out from the crowd on numerous occasions. Fear of embarrassment holds us back and prevents us from achieving what we are truly capable of.

In 1999, I played at Wembley Stadium for England Schoolboys against Hungry U18s. It was a massive day in my life as all my friends and family were there in attendance. We travelled by coach to the game via a police escort; the stadium was packed with 36,000 people and this was by far the largest crowd I had ever played in front of. As we arrived at Wembley I imagined all the stars that had played on the hallowed turf. I could quite clearly recall attending a Wembley Stadium tour two years prior to our game; during the tour I was forced to stand on the other side of the "Keep off the Pitch" sign, and now here I was walking around pitch-side with total freedom. As the game was drawing closer, a parade started to take place on the pitch, consisting of fireworks and a large brass band; this meant that we didn't get to run onto the pitch until just before kickoff, so we warmed up in the tunnel. As the time came for us to eventually run out onto the pitch, heavy rain starting pouring down. The old Wembley still had a metal run-up to the side of the pitch; I had metal studs on and was very excited to get onto the freshly cut grass. As I jogged out of the tunnel, I heard a loud roar from the crowd and I felt like a million dollars. This feeling was very abruptly replaced by shock. A chorus of laughter sounded around the stadium as the crowd laughed in unison at me: I had slipped and hit the floor. How embarrassing that, in front of all these people, my studs had given way on the metal railing and I had tripped and subsequently crashed to the ground. This one event could have destroyed my confidence—after all, I was about to play in the biggest game of my life—but it didn't. I brushed myself down, got up, smiled and then waved at the crowd as they cheered me once again. Well, do you know what happened next? I went out onto that pitch and had my best game in an England shirt and despite our 1–0 loss, I received "Star Man" in a number of the national papers the very next day.

The fall eradicated all my nerves for the game; after all, how could it get any worse after that? I was able to play with a sense of freedom, perspective and, more importantly, enjoyment. A similar thing happened while I was playing at youth team level (U18s) for Leyton Orient. I was driving to a game in East London; on the way there I crashed my car for the very first time in my life. I drove into the back of another vehicle and wrote my car off. I managed to get a lift to the game from another player. I felt strange in the car as we neared the football ground. I started the game and again played without any fear; after all, I could have broken my legs two hours earlier, and I even scored one of the best goals of my career from the halfway line. I know that without that crash I wouldn't have dreamed of attempting to chip the keeper from that range, but the crash gave me a sense of bravery to try things outside the realm of my normal capabilities. It's amazing how many times trying things outside the deemed norm of society pays off. Some accomplishments are only achievable if, in the short term, you lose the fear of what others are thinking or saying.

I believe thinking about being old or even dying eradicates that fear. Fear can control you or you can control it; it's a conscious decision. A life lived with fear doesn't sound that enjoyable to me. If you agree, start taking steps to squash it. What is your biggest fear? What are the chances of this happening? What if I told you that you have absolutely no control over this event occurring!? Whether you pray, think positively or negatively or kiss your lucky rabbit's foot, this event will either happen or not, but you will have no say in this—none whatsoever. You need to start to control what you can and leave what you can't. If you are able to do this, then your life will automatically consist of less worry and stress. The happiest people live in the moment; they have a long-term goal and passion that they are striving for, but essentially, they control what they can along the way and let go of what they can't.

It's like boarding a plane. I have developed a worry of flying as I've gotten older. I think this was established during my time in America, where we would fly in smaller aircrafts between states for the San Jose State University soccer team. The small plane would rattle around and I'm sure I remember seeing chicken coops on one flight. I have learnt that any single flight, that we have no control over, is either going to land safely or crash. We can either stress about the flight all the way to our destination or sit back and enjoy a bloody Mary—for some reason I only drink these when I fly. I opt for the bloody Mary route; it seems to be working out much better for me.

The power of facing your fears and overcoming them is a huge self-esteem boost. If you've ever heard or read about a near-death experience or of somebody being announced clinically dead for a set amount of time, you will know that once they come out the other side of this ordeal, they are a different person. What's changed? Perspective. Have you ever hit the snooze button on your alarm and dragged yourself out your bed, started getting ready for work and then realised it's a bank holiday or even a Sunday!? I'm sure, in this moment, you will experience a feeling of relief and maybe even delight, no matter how much you love and enjoy your job.

How we perceive the world around us is the only factor that affects thoughts and, therefore, our feelings. Whether it's a bank holiday, a Monday or a Friday, there is no change in the physical world apart from our reaction to a stimulus which is then perceived positively or negatively. If you were to drop your phone on the ground and it broke, it is only your perception of this accident that affects your feelings. This could devastate one person, yet another person may not even give it a second thought. It's the same event, just perceived differently. Perspective is a key term in life and your perspective can affect your view. Remember, the larger the picture you see, the greater perspective you possess.

Imagine waking up in a hospital bed surrounded

by nurses and your family. **"You have been dead for one minute!"** they tell you. As this news sinks in, you realize you know everybody in the room apart from who you are. In one scenario, the nurse tells you that you are a war hero and you have saved the lives of hundreds of men, you have an MBE from the Queen and currently you are on the front page of many national newspapers. In Scenario 2 you awaken and are told that you work in a supermarket, you have just found a job after being homeless for nearly a year and you are also overcoming a drug addiction. How would you feel in each scenario? How would you carry yourself? Our internal voice and self-perception greatly affect our perspective of self-worth and self-value. How we feel about events within our lives is dependent upon our perception. For greater perception, try to imagine yourself looking back on your life.

Lesson: Embarrassment and fear are negative emotions; they can control and ruin lives. Once you eradicate this way of thinking from your life, you can become free to attempt new experiences, and to start to achieve in all areas of your life. Spend some time fast-forwarding to an older version of yourself; this will help you to reflect on what you really want to accomplish and be remembered for. Once you decide on your inner desires, then you must find the courage to proceed. The "older you" will regret it otherwise. Imagine the grim reaper came calling tomorrow—morbid I know, but what desires buried in your heart would you want to complete? Ultimately, when our time is up, the fact that we did or didn't follow our true heart's desires is all that really matters.

Key Words:

Reflect * Regret * Time * Proactive
*Heart *Perception

Quiz

1) If Indiana Jones was actually afraid of facing a challenge, then what would the films have been about?
2) What fear did Batman overcome to turn into a real strength of his?
3) What would the world be like without Facebook and Reality TV?
4) What would the world be like without moaners and groaners?
5) What is the maximum amount of time you can spend laughing in any given day?
6) When is the best time to exercise?
7) Who we do sometimes treat the worst but love the most?
8) Which group of people do we smile at the most?
9) Time travel ... when do we want it?
10) Who is the greatest time traveller of all time?

Answers

1) *An interesting four part documentary on university lecturing*

2) *Wearing black leather*

3) *Better*

4) *Much better*

5) *Unlimited (unless, of course, you are at a serious event or in class—then do it quietly!)*

6) *The morning, afternoon, evening, mid-morning or at night ... whenever!*

7) *Family*

8) *Bar staff (Anything to get served a bit quicker!)*

9) *It's irrelevant!*

10) *The one and only Doctor Emmett Brown ... FACT.*

Reality Refreshed

Opportunity Knocks

As we start the last leg of our journey together I hope that you have been able to put into practice some of the 5 codes. A shift in perception is a powerful thing, for there is no greater sight than a person with a passion and self-belief in action. I want you to find that purpose; it is essential for progress to take place. Start attempting smaller challenges, and then you can build from this foundation. However, whatever your passion may be, do not quit or decrease your motivation in its pursuit, for this is the easy option. Leave fear behind as you sign up to a new class or begin a new project; put yourself out there and engage with others who share similar interests. Small steps lead to larger changes and, with commitment, over time, anything is possible.

I have refreshed my life by adhering to these five codes; through them, I have dramatically progressed both physically and mentally. The initial step for me was to decide to start exercising outdoors, away from the confines of a gym or health club. After a debilitating back injury, I slowly found a new love in calisthenics, a form of body-weight exercise. Self-improvement solely using this form of training took time, effort and focus. Nonetheless, I committed everything I had to one idea, an idea that still burns away at me today: **Be better than you were yesterday**.

I dragged this philosophy into other areas of my life. I opted to start reading to improve my mental development and cognitive functioning, quickly witnessing an increase in my vocabulary and input in discussions. The self-development improved my confidence; hence, I became increasingly positive about my life and circumstances. As I radiated new positivity into the universe, further opportunities opened up to me. The additional opportunities that I acted upon provided me with personal growth and development. It is without exaggeration that I say the five codes have changed my life. I was down and out, drifting through life and not heading in the direction I was destined to. The universe intervened and encouraged me to refresh my reality and, therefore, my mindset. In essence, I was forced to rebuild my personal belief system from the foundation up. I am thankful for all the adversity in my life as it has facilitated my evolution into the person I am destined to be and intent on becoming.

Code 1: Learn to Love Negative Experiences

Negative experiences such as failure and disappointment are all part of the process to achieving your innermost dreams. It is your ability to remain steadfast and endeavour through these ordeals that will, just like natural selection, create a stronger version of you.

Code 2: Meet Your New Drug Dealers: Laughter & Exercise

Visit these two characters, laughter and exercise, as often as you can. Being a physically stronger version of yourself will impact all areas of your life, including the ability to sleep, learn and focus, while laughter will keep you in the present moment.

Code 3: Zoom Out to See the Bigger Picture

Find a purpose and a passion that enables you to focus on the bigger picture. Ignore the daily negative distractions and people that can drown your ambition. Thrive with a purpose.

Code 4: Family & Friends Before All Else

Family should always be your main priority. Get to know them, understand their views and always show them respect. The quality of the friendships and the bonds that you create along your journey through life will depict everything about you and your character. Trust people, show kindness where you can and forgive often.

Code 5: Tales of a Time Traveller

Fast-forward in time to analyse the outcomes of your decisions and life. Will the future you be proud of the pathway you're currently taking? What will you remember and be remembered for? Time is the most valuable currency we possess. Do not waste it on anything other than the pursuit of your heart's desires.

Final Lesson:

Go out and be a go-getter. Be someone who is not afraid to fail over and over again, because you are aware that every failure is helping you to evolve and adapt. There is nothing as precious as right now, so stop wasting time on anything or anyone that doesn't bring positivity to your existence. If you can, try to fill your life with positive, progressive people. People may not understand the journey you are about to embark on. The easiest solution to non-code followers is to complain or put down from afar. You must ignore these people.

Challenge yourself to read more and expand your mind. Become physically active and promote a healthy lifestyle for yourself and others. We all have very different talents; it may take time for you to truly find yours, but don't be afraid to step away from the crowd. How are your decisions going to appear when you look back on your life? Will you have any regrets? You have the time machine at your disposal, and this will help you to fully prepare for being an older version of yourself. However, today—yes, today—you have started becoming a stronger version of yourself.

Follow these five codes and witness changes start to surface in your thinking and appearance. We will never be the finished article. The expansion of the mind and the body doesn't have a sell-by date. Life is about continuing to learn and grow.

Homework

Please complete the homework set below. Who knows what path this will lead you on...

- **Resources.** You will need to purchase a blank notebook or continue with the one you have used for previous tasks.

- **Goals.** List your three goals from <u>Task 1</u> on the inside cover, e.g.:

<u>My Goals</u>
I want to learn a new language
I want to find a new job
I want to start to read a book once a week

- **Inspiration.** Beneath these goals, now list the three people from <u>Task 4</u> who have had a positive effect on your life, e.g.:

> **My Inspiration**
> Mum
> Uncle John
> My first teacher

- **Report-writing**. This notebook is now going to be important in your development and progress. You will list anything and everything in it. You may wish to complete some research into your goals. Discover what's involved in achieving them and how you can get started. Plan a pathway to success using useful websites, contact numbers, new ideas, and things you need to improve, e.g.:

> **Week 1:**
> 1) I have bought a "Learn Spanish" CD. I plan on listening to this in the mornings on my train journey into work. By Day 5 I want to be able to order tapas from a restaurant.
> 2) I have also started to complete my CV and I am researching recruitment companies to send this to. I want to have this complete by 23/11/2016.
> 3) I am going to ask Kate at work if she has

> any books she can recommend as I know she likes to read; maybe I will join the local library.

- **Regrets.** Place the two events from your experience in the time machine for **Task 5** in a place where you will see them every day. This could be on your fridge, on a notice board, on the front or back cover of the notebook or as a screenshot on your phone.

- **Year Review.** Plan to set aside some time one year on from the date you signed your written agreement. This will be used to reflect and review progress towards your goals. Place this date in your diary or set a reminder on your phone. During this yearly review, you will also set some new goals that build on your previous year's endeavours. Quitting is the easiest thing to do. You will be tempted, but sometimes the best thing for you is also the most difficult. Maintaining these codes for the first year is the hardest thing to do. However, if you complete a year of code-following, I guarantee a happier, more confident and content you in twelve months' time.

- **Funny Memories**. Lastly, if possible, I want you to call or email the people involved in the funny stories that you listed in **Task 2** and reminisce about the incidents. Why? So you can enjoy these moments again. Additionally, laughter will provide you with a small dose of endorphins for your trouble.

Habits will take four to six weeks to form and become part of your daily routine. Habitual behaviour eventually becomes the foundation of who you are and what you represent, so allow this time period for new positive behaviours to fully embed. Your notebook will become your personal solution for positive change; refer to it daily and record the progress you experience.

If I could leave you with a final idea or concept, it would be to consider what you truly want out of life and whether this vision conflicts with your current daily habits. If you are not working towards what you truly desire, then by default you are not heading in the direction of your dreams. We are all in this present moment together; some people seize each moment while others let them drift by. At any given moment you have the power to say: **"this is not how** my story is going to end!" Indeed, 50 percent of readers will take up these codes, witnessing improvements within their lives. The remaining 50 percent of people will put this book down and decline any attempt to change. Within a month they will be searching bookstores or the Internet again for further self-help techniques. These codes work, if you commit to them.

Final Challenge

To signify the completion of this book and your initiation as a fellow code-follower, you have one last bonus task. I want you to walk into your kitchen and find a piece of china you hate (or just mildly dislike). This could be a bowl, a plate or a mug. Proceed to take the object outside to a concrete area and drop it. That's right, drop it and watch it smash. In Greek culture, the voluntary breaking of plates is a form of controlled loss. You are now taking control of your own destiny. Your loss is the old you and the negative way of thinking. The broken pieces represent the confined version of you. As you clear up the pieces and throw them away, say goodbye to your old way of thinking and living. Feel the freedom of the new you as you start to perceive the world differently. This task is essential. Just like your past school lessons, you will remember a unique or exceptional moment over countless monotonous ones. Put simply, this final task will help you to remember and embed the five codes uncovered throughout the previous chapters.

You are now ready to dive into life and
Start Swimming...

On a Personal Note

Thank you very much for purchasing my first published book. You have helped me to complete one of my life goals. I truly hope you find it beneficial in your current circumstance. I also pray that you continue the pursuit of becoming a better version of yourself.

Writing this book has forced me to reflect on my own life and furthermore, my long term goals. I have taken the opportunity to hop in the time machine; with this experience, I have discovered a hidden aspiration of my own. I now know that I have an inner desire to travel across America. I have always wanted to complete Route 66 on Harley Davison Motorbike.

So, I'm off to plan my next adventure........

Good Luck & Best Wishes

Peter James Barkley

NetKandi Media & Publishing

References & Further Reading

Physical activity moderates effects of stressor-induced rumination on cortisol reactivity. Puterman E[1], O'Donovan A, Adler NE, Tomiyama AJ, Kemeny M, Wolkowitz OM, Epel E. {Psychosom Med. 2011 Sep;73(7):604-11. doi: 10.1097/PSY.0b013e318229e1e0 }

Cortisol, serotonin and depression: all stressed out? By P.J. COWEN {The British Journal of Psychiatry Feb 2002, 180 (2) 99-100; **DOI:** 10.1192/bjp.180.2.99}

How to Win Friends & Influence People by Dale Carnegie

Mindset: How You Can Fulfil Your Potential Paperback – 2 Feb 2012 by Carol Dweck (Author)

Spark: The Revolutionary New Science of Exercise and the Brain by John J. Ratey,

The 9 Cardinal Building Blocks: For Continued Success in Leadership by Assegid Habtewold

The Power of Positive Thinking by Norman Vincent Peale,

Unapologetically You: Reflections on Life and the Human Experience by Steve Maraboli

Why We Work by Barry Schwartz